The Kumulipo

The Kumulipo

Lili'uokalani

MINT EDITIONS

The *Kumulipo* was first published in 1897.

This edition published by Mint Editions 2021.

ISBN 9781513299556 | E-ISBN 9781513223858

Published by Mint Editions®

MINT
EDITIONS

minteditionbooks.com

Publishing Director: Jennifer Newens
Design & Production: Rachel Lopez Metzger
Project Manager: Micaela Clark
Typesetting: Westchester Publishing Services

He Pule Hoolaa Alii

(An ancient prayer for the dedication of the high chief
Lonoikamakahiki to the gods, soon after his birth, and at
which time the honors of Kapu, Wela, Hoano, and Moe
were conferred on him by his father, Keaweikekahialiiokamoku,
King of Hawaii. After the ceremony his name was
changed to Ka I i Mamao.)

He Kumulipo
(The Creation)
For
Ka I I Mamao
From Him to His Daughter, Alapai Wahine.

Contents

Introduction 9

The First Era, or Age 13

The Second Era 18

The Third Era 24

The Fourth Era 28

The Fifth Era 32

The Sixth Era 34

The Seventh Era 35

The Eighth Era 36

The Ninth Era 38

The Tenth Era 39

The Eleventh Era 40

The Twelfth Era 69

A Branch of the Twelfth Era 76

The Fourteenth Era 79

The Fifteenth Era 83

The Sixteenth Era 86

INTRODUCTION

There are several reasons for the publication of this work, the translation of which pleasantly employed me while imprisoned by the present rulers of Hawaii. It will be to my friends a souvenir of that part of my own life, and possibly it may also be of value to genealogists and scientific men of a few societies to which a copy will be forwarded. The folk-lore or traditions of an aboriginal people have of late years been considered of inestimable value; language itself changes, and there are terms and allusions herein to the natural history of Hawaii, which might be forgotten in future years without some such history as this to preserve them to posterity. Further, it is the special property of the latest ruling family of the Hawaiian Islands, being nothing less than the genealogy in remote times of the late King Kalakaua,—who had it printed in the original Hawaiian language,—and myself.

This is the very chant which was sung by Puou, the High Priest of our ancient worship, to Captain Cook whom they had surnamed Lono, one of the four chief gods, dwelling high in the heavens, but at times appearing on the earth. This was the cause of the deification of Captain Cook under that name, and of the offerings to him made at the temple or Heiau at Hikiau, Kealakekua, where this song was rendered.

Captain Cook's appearance was regarded by our people then as a confirmation of their own traditions. For it was prophesied by priests at the time of the death of Ka-I-i-mamao that he, Lono, would return anew from the sea in a Spanish man-of-war or Auwaalalua. To the great navigator they accordingly gave a welcome with the name of Lono.

The chanters of this great poem were Hewahewa and Ahukai, and by them it was originally dedicated to Alapai, our ancestress, a woman-chief of the highest rank, then at Koko Oahu. Keeaumoku was lying on his death-bed. The Lonoikamakahiki, of whom this chant sings so eloquently in our native tongue, is none other than Kalaninuiiamamao (Ka-I-i-mamao). His name was also Lonoikamakahiki. He was thus called by his mother, Lonomaikanaka, from the very moment of his birth. It was his grandmother Keakealani who changed his name at the time he was dedicated to the gods and the sacred tabus of the Wela, Hoano, and the Moe; or, translated, Fire, Honor, and Adoration were conferred upon him at the time when his navel string was cut at the Heiau at Nueku, Kahaluu, Kona, Hawaii. The correct name of this chief was Ka-I-i-mamao, but the bards of his day named him in their chants Kalaninuiiamamao; thus he was styled in their Mele or chant called Kekoauli-kookea ka lani. The words "lani nui" were simply inserted by them as it was their intention to hand the young prince's name down to posterity in song, while to explain the object of the parents in naming him Ka-I-i-mamao it signified that when Keawe married Lonoma-I-Kanaka it was an infusion of a new royal blood with that of their own royal line of I, the father of Ahu, the grandfather of Lonomaikanaka. By this it was also intended to show that he, that is Ka-I-i-mamao, was above all other I's, for there were many families, descendants of I, a high and powerful chief, and the last term, "mamao," means "far off" and above all the rest of the I's.

Before he was deposed by the people of Kau he was called Wakea on account of his wicked actions, and, like Wakea, he married his own daughter. By this name he wandered through the wilds of Kahihikolo at Kalihikai, Kalihiwai, and Hanalei, and ultimately became demented. Through all his wanderings he was followed by his faithful attendant and retainer Kapaihi a Hilina.

This historical character is distinct from the Lonoikamakahiki, son of Keawenuiaumi, the same one who challenged

Kakuhihewa at checkers, Konane. He figured at a different period. There were really three persons of the name of Lonoikamakahiki; the first of these was the son of Keawenuiaumi; the second was a celebrated hunchback son of Kapulehuwaihele, and belonged to Makakaualii. The third Lonoikamakahiki is the one for whom this prayer was composed. His parents were Keaweikekahialiiokamoku and Lonomaikaamaka. Ka-I-i-mamao was the father of Kalaniopuu, this last-named being ancestor in the third degree of King Kalakaua, who reigned over the Hawaiian kingdom from 1874 to 1891, and of Lili'uokalani, who reigned from 1891 to 1893. He was also ancestor in second and third degree to the wife of Kalakaua, at present the dowager Queen Kapiolani.

It will be seen, therefore, that as connecting the earlier kings of ancient history with the monarchs latest upon the throne this chant is a contribution to the history of the Hawaiian Islands, and as it is the only record of its kind in existence it seemed to me worthy of preservation in convenient form.

I have endeavored to give the definition of each name as far as it came within my knowledge of words, but in some cases this could not be done because the true signification has been lost. The ancient

Hawaiians were astronomers, and the terms used appertained to the heavens, the stars, terrestrial science, and the gods. Curious students will notice in this chant analogies between its accounts of the creation and that given by modern science or Sacred Scripture. As with other religions, our ancient people recognized an all-powerful evil spirit: Mea was the King of Milu as Satan is of the infernal regions, or hell.

I hope that to some interested in all that pertains to Hawaii, this may give one-half the pleasure which it gave to me in the translation and preparation of the manuscript.

LILI‘UOKALANI, *of Hawaii,*
Patron of the Polynesian Historical Society

The First Era, or Age

First Verse

At the time that turned the heat of the earth,
At the time when the heavens turned and changed,
At the time when the light of the sun was subdued
To cause light to break forth,
At the time of the night of Makalii (winter)
Then began the slime which established the earth,
The source of deepest darkness.
Of the depth of darkness, of the depth of darkness,
Of the darkness of the sun, in the depth of night,
It is night,
So was night born.

Second Verse

Kumulipo was born in the night, a male.
Poele was born in the night, a female.
A coral insect was born, from which was born perforated coral.
The earth worm was born, which gathered earth into mounds,
From it were born worms full of holes.
The starfish was born, whose children were born starry.
The phosphorous was born, whose children were born
   phosphorescent.
The Iua was born Ina (sea egg).
The Halula was born Halula (sea urchin).
Shell-fish.
The Hawae was born, the Wana-ku was its offspring.
The Haukeuke was born, the Uhalula was its offspring.
The Pioe was born, the Pipi was its offspring (clam oyster).
The Papaua was born, the Olepe was its offspring (pearl and oyster).
The Nahawele was born, the Unauna was its offspring (muscle and
   crab in a shell).
The Makaiaulu was born, the Opihi was its offspring.
The Leho was born, the Puleholeho was its offspring (cowry).
The Naka was born, its offspring was Kupekala (rock oysters).

The Makaloa was born, the Pupuawa was its offspring.
The Ole was born, the Oleole was its offspring (conch).
The Pipipi was born, the Kupee was its offspring (limpets).

Kane was born to Waiololi, a female to Waiolola.
The Wi was born, the Kiki was its offspring.
The Akaha's home was the sea;
Guarded by the Ekahakaha that grew in the forest.
A night of flight by noises
Through a channel; water is life to trees;
So the gods may enter, but not man.

Third Verse

Seaweed and grasses
Man by Waiololi, woman by Waiolola,
The Akiaki was born and lived in the sea;
Guarded by the Manienie Akiaki that grew in the forest.
A night of flight by noises
Through a channel; water is life to trees;
So the gods may enter, but not man.

Fourth Verse

Man by Waiololi, woman by Waiolola,
The Aalaula was born and lived in the sea;
Guarded by the Alaalawainui that grew in the forest.
A night of flight by noises
Through a channel; water is life to trees;
So the gods may enter, but not man.

Fifth Verse

Man by Waiololi, woman by Waiolola,
The Manauea was born and lived in the sea;
Guarded by the Kalo Manauea that grew in the forest.
A night of flight by noises
Through a channel; water is life to trees;
So the gods may enter, but not man.

Sixth Verse

Seaweed and grasses
Man by Waiololi, woman by Waiolola,
The Koeleele was born and lived in the sea;
Guarded by the Ko punapuna Koeleele that grew in the forest.
A night of flight by noises
Through a channel; water is life to trees;
So the gods may enter, but not man.

Seventh Verse

Man by Waiololi, woman by Waiolola,
The Puaiki was born and lived in the sea;
Guarded by the Lauaki that grew in the forest.
A night of flight by noises
Through a channel; water is life to trees;
So the gods may enter, but not man.

Eighth Verse

Man by Waiololi, woman by Waiolola,
The Kikalamoa was born and lived in the sea;
Guarded by the Moamoa that grew in the forest.
A night of flight by noises
Through a channel; water is life to trees;
So the gods may enter, but not man.

Ninth Verse

Man by Waiololi, woman by Waiolola,
The Limukele was born and lived in the sea;
Guarded by the Ekele that grew in the forest.
A night of flight by noises
Through a channel; water is life to trees;
So the gods may enter, but not man.

Tenth Verse

Man by Waiololi, woman by Waiolola,
The Limukala was born and lived in the sea;
Guarded by the Akala that grew in the forest.
A night of flight by noises
Through a channel; water is life to trees;
So the gods may enter, but not man.

Eleventh Verse

Man by Waiololi, woman by Waiolola,
The Lipuupuu was born and lived in the sea;
Guarded by the Lipuu that grew in the forest.
A night of flight by noises
Through a channel; water is life to trees;
So the gods may enter but not man.

Twelfth Verse

Seaweed and grasses
Man by Waiololi, woman by Waiolola,
The Loloa was born and lived in the sea;
Guarded by the Kalamaloloa that grew in the forest.
A night of flight by noises
Through a channel; water is life to trees;
So the gods may enter, but not man.

Thirteenth Verse

Seaweed and grasses
Man by Waiololi, woman by Waiolola,
The Ne was born and lived in the sea;
Guarded by the Neneleau that grew in the forest.
A night of flight by noises
Through a channel; water is life to trees;
So the gods may enter, but not man.

Fourteenth Verse

Man by Waiololi, woman by Waiolola,
The Hulu-waena was born and lived in the sea;
Guarded by the Huluhulu Ieie that grew in the forest.
A night of flight by noises
Through a channel; water is life to trees;
So the gods may enter, but not man.

Fifteenth Verse

A husband of gourd, and yet a god,
A tendril strengthened by water and grew
A being, produced by earth and spread,
Made deafening by the swiftness of Time
Of the Hee that lengthened through the night,
That filled and kept on filling
Of filling, until, filled
To filling, 'tis full,
And supported the earth, which held the heaven
On the wing of Time, the night is for Kumulipo (creation),
                    'Tis night.

The Second Era

First Verse

The first child born of Powehiwehi (dusky night)
Tossed up land for Pouliuli (darkest night),
For Mahiuma or Maapuia,
And lived in the land of Pohomiluamea (sloughy hill of Mea);
Suppressed the noise of the growth of unripe fruit,
For fear Uliuli would cause it to burst, and the stench
To disagree and turn sour,
For pits of darkness and pits of night.
Then the seven waters became calm.
Then was born a child (kama), 'twas a Hilu and swam.
The Hilu is a fish with standing fins,
On which Pouliuli sat.
So undecided seemed Powehiwehi,
For Pouliuli was husband
And Powehiwehi his wife.

Fish.

And fish was born, the Naia (porpoise) was born in the sea and swam.
The Mano (shark) was born, the Moana was born in the sea and swam.
The Mau was born, the Maumau was born in the sea and swam.
The Nana was born, the Mana was born in the sea and swam.
The Nake was born, the Make was born in the sea and swam.
The Napa was born, the Nala was born in the sea and swam.
The Pala was born, the Kala was born in the sea and swam.
The Paka (an eel) was born, the Papa (crab) was born in the sea and swam.
The Kalakala was born, the Huluhulu was born in the sea and swam.
The Halahala was born, the Palapala was born in the sea and swam.
The Pea (starfish) was born, the Lupe was born in the sea and swam.
The Ao was born, the Awa was born in the sea and swam.
The Aku (bonito) was born, the Ahi (same kind) was born in the sea and swam.
The Opelu (same as above) was born, the Akule was born in the sea and swam.

The Amaama (mullet) was born, the Anae (large kind) was born in the sea and swam.
The Ehu was born, the Nehu was born in the sea and swam.
The Iao (used for bait) was born, the Aoao was born in the sea and swam.
The Ono (large fish) was born, the Omo was born in the sea and swam.
The Pahau (striped flatfish) was born, the Lauhau was born in the sea and swam.
The Moi was born, the Loiloi was born in the sea and swam.
The Mao was born, the Maomao was born in the sea and swam.
The Kaku was born, the A'ua'u was born in the sea and swam.
The Kupou was born, the Kupoupou was born in the sea and swam.
The Weke was born, the Lele was born in the sea and swam.
The Palani was born, the Nuku Moni was born in the sea and swam.
The Ulua was born, the Hahalua was born in the sea and swam.
The Aoaonui was born, the Pakukui was born in the sea and swam.
The Maiii was born, the Alaihi was born in the sea and swam.
The Oo was born, the Akilolo was born in the sea and swam.

Second Verse

Fish and vine.
The Nenue was born and lived in the sea;
Guarded by the Lauhue that grew in the forest.
A night of flight by noises
Through a channel; salt water is life to fish;
So the gods may enter, but not man.

Third Verse

Fish and vine.
Man by Waiololi, woman by Waiolola,
The Haha was born and lived in the sea;
Guarded by the Puhala that grew in the forest.
A night of flight by noises
Through a channel; salt water is life to fish;
So the gods may enter, but not man.

Fish and shrub.
Man by Waiololi, woman by Waiolola,
The Pahau was born in the sea;
Guarded by the Lauhau that grew in the forest.
A night of flight by noises
Through a channel; salt water is life to fish;
So the gods may enter, but not man.

FIFTH VERSE

Fish and shrub.
Man by Waiololi, woman by Waiolola,
The Hee was born and lived in the sea;
Guarded by the Walahee that grew in the forest.
A night of flight by noises
Through a channel; salt water is life to fish;
So the gods may enter, but not man.

SIXTH VERSE

Sea and water fish.
Man by Waiololi, woman by Waiolola,
The Oopukai was born and lived in the sea;
Guarded by the Oopuwai that lived in the forest.
A night of flight by noises
Through a channel; salt water is life to fish;
So the gods may enter, but not man.

SEVENTH VERSE

Eel and tree.
Man by Waiololi, woman by Waiolola,
The Puhi kauwila was born and lived in the sea;
Guarded by the Uwila that lived in the forest.
A night of flight by noises
Through a channel; salt water is life to fish;
So the gods may enter, but not man.

EIGHTH VERSE

Fish and bread-fruit.
Man by Waiololi, woman by Waiolola,
The Umaumalei was born and lived in the sea;
Guarded by the Ulei that grew in the forest.
A night of flight by noises
Through a channel; salt water is life to fish;
So the gods may enter, but not man.

NINTH VERSE

Eel and tree.
Man by Waiololi, woman by Waiolola,
The Pakukui was born and lived in the sea;
Guarded by Laukukui that grew in the forest.
A night of flight by noises
Through a channel; salt water is life to fish;
So the gods may enter, but not man.

TENTH VERSE

Eel and tree.
Man by Waiololi, woman by Waiolola,
The Laumilo was born and lived in the sea;
Guarded by the Milo that grew in the forest.
A night of flight by noises
Through a channel; salt water is life to fish;
So the gods may enter, but not man.

ELEVENTH VERSE

Fish and large tree.
Man by Waiololi, woman by Waiolola,
The Kapoou was born and lived in the sea;
Guarded by Kou that grew in the forest.
A night of flight by noises
Through a channel; salt water is life to fish;
So the gods may enter, but not man.

Twelfth Verse

Fish and yam or Uhi
(Impomea batatas).
Man by Waiololi, woman by Waiolola,
The Hauliuli was born and lived in the sea;
Guarded by the Uhi that grew in the forest.
A night of flight by noises
Through a channel; water is life to fish;
So the gods may enter, but not man.

Thirteenth Verse

Man by Waiololi, woman by Waiolola,
The Weke was born and lived in the sea;
Guarded by the Wauke that grew in the forest.
A night of flight by noises
Through a channel; water is life to fish;
So the gods may enter, but not man.

Fourteenth Verse

Fish and Awa
(Kawa).
Man by Waiololi, woman by Waiolola,
The Aawa was born and lived in the sea;
Guarded by the Awa that grew in the forest.
A night of flight by noises
Through a channel; water is life to fish;
So the gods may enter, but not man.

Fifteenth Verse

Fish and grass.
Man by Waiololi, woman by Waiolola,
The Ulae was born and lived in the sea;
Guarded by the Mokae that grew in the forest.
A night of flight by noises

Through a channel; salt water is life to fish;
So the gods may enter, but not man.

Sixteenth Verse

Man by Waiololi, woman by Waiolola,
The Palaoa (sea-elephant) was born and lived in the sea;
Guarded by the Aoa that grew in the forest.
A night of flight by noises
Through a channel; salt water is life to fish;
So the gods may enter, but not man.

Seventeenth Verse

The train of Palaoa (walrus) that swim by
Embracing only the deep blue waters,
Also the Opule that move in schools,
The deep is as nothing to them.
And the Kumimi (a crab) and Lohelohe (a locust) cling together
To the rolling motion of their cradle
On their path so narrow, so slim, to move,
Till Pimoe (a mermaid) is found in the depth of her cave,
With Hikawainui, and Hikawaina
Amongst piles of heated coral
That were thrown in piles unevenly,
So thin and scraggy in the blue tide.
Surely it must be dismal, that unknown deep;
'Tis a sea of coral from the depth of Paliuli,
And when the land recedes from them
The east is still in darkness of night,
       'Tis night.

The Third Era

First Verse

He was the man and she the woman;
The man that was born in the dark age,
And the woman was born in the age of bubbles.
The sea spread, the land spread,
The waters spread, the mountains spread,
The Poniu grew tall with advancing time,
The Haha grew and had nine leaves,
And the Palai (fern) sprout that shot forth leaves of high chiefs
Brought forth Poeleele, a man (darkness),
Who lived with Pohaha, a woman (bubbles),
And brought forth generations of Haha (kalo tops).
                    The Haha was born.

Second Verse

Insects.
The Haha was born and became parent;
His offspring, a Hahalelelele, was born.
The Peelua (caterpillar) was born and became parent;
Its offspring was a flying Pulelehua (butterfly).
The Naonao (an ant) was born and became parent;
Its offspring was a Pinao (dragonfly).
The Unia was born and became parent;
Its offspring was an Uhini, and flew (grasshopper).
The Naio was born and became parent (waterworms);
Its offspring was a Nalo, and flew (flies).
                    Birds.
The Hualua was born and became parent;
Its offspring was a bird, and flew.
The Ulili was born and became parent (snipe);
Its offspring was a Kolea, and flew (plover).
The A-o was born and became parent;
Its offspring was an Au, and flew (a species of plover).

The Akekeke was born and became parent (sea-bird);
Its offspring was Elepaio, and flew (woodpecker).
The Alae was born and became parent (mud hen);
Its offspring was an Apapane, and flew (red woodpecker).
The Alala was born and became parent (crow);
Its offspring was an Alawi, and flew.
The Eea was born and became parent;
Its offspring was a Alaiaha, and flew.
The Mamo was born and became parent (the royal bird);
Its offspring was the Oo, and flew (black woodpecker).
The Moha was born and became parent (wingless bird);
Its offspring was a Moli, and flew.
Sea-birds.

The Kiki was born and became parent;
Its offspring was the Ukihi, and flew.
The Kioea was born and became parent (stork);
Its offspring was a Kukuluaeo, and flew (crane).
The Ka Iwa was born and became parent (sea-bird);
Its offspring was a Koae, and flew (man-of-war hawk).
The Kala was born and became parent (sea-bird);
Its offspring was a Kaula, and flew (sea-bird).
Then was born the Unauna (shell-fish, part crab);
Its offspring was an Aukuu, and flew.

> These birds fly together in flocks
> And usually light on the sea beach
> And array themselves in line.

THIRD VERSE

They covered the land of Kanehunamoku.
These were born birds of the land
And birds of the sea.
Man was born of Waiololi, woman Waiolola,
The Lupe was born and lived in the sea;
Guarded by the Lupe that grew in the forest.
A night of flight by noises
Through a channel; the Io is life to birds;
So the gods may enter, but not man.

Fourth Verse

Man by Waiololi, woman by Waiolola,
The Noio lived on the sea,
Guarded by the Io that lived in the forest.
A night of flight by noises.
Eggs and the Io are life to birds,
So the gods may enter, but not man.

Fifth Verse

Man by Waiololi, woman by Waiolola,
The Kolea of the island lived on the sea,
Guarded by the Kolea that flew on land.
A night of flight by noises.
Eggs and Io are life to birds,
So the gods may enter, but not man.

Sixth Verse

Man by Waiololi, woman by Waiolola,
The Hehe was born and lived on the sea,
Guarded by the Nene that lived in the forest.
A night of flight by noises.
Eggs and Io are life to birds,
So the gods may enter, but not man.

Seventh Verse

Man by Waiololi, woman by Waiolola,
The Aukuu was born and lived on the sea (Pewit),
Guarded by the Ekupuu that grew on land.
A night of flight by noises.
Eggs and Io are life to birds,
So the gods may enter, but not man.

Eighth Verse

Man by Waiololi, woman by Waiolola,
The Noeo was born and lived on the sea,
Guarded by the Pueo that lived in the forest.
A night of flight by noises.
Eggs and Io are food for birds,
So the gods may enter, but not man.

Ninth Verse

This is the leaping point of the bird Halulu
Of Kiwaa, the bird of many notes,
And of those birds that fly closely together as to shade the sun,
They cover the land with their young to the rock's edge,
Their gall burst easily with a smack
As the Ape sprout whose delicate shoots
Shoot forth their young sprouts and spread
And bring forth in their birth many branches.
    It was so on that night,
    It was so this night,
    It was dark at the time with Poeleele,
    And darkest age—of bubbly night.
      'Tis night.

THE FOURTH ERA

FIRST VERSE

Established in the dawn of Laa's light
The Ape aumoa with faintest strife
Envied the sea that washed the land,
As it crept up and yet crept down
And brought forth creeping families
That crept on their backs and crept on their front,
With pulses that beat in front and rounding backs,
With faces in front and claws to feel
Of darkness, of darkness,
For Kaneaka Papanopano is born (dawn).
So Popanopano the man
And Polalowehi his wife,
Man was born to increase—
To increase in the night by the thousands.
At this age there is a lull—
At this age take your children to the beach.
Children play at heaping sands.
They are the children born of night.
Night was born.

SECOND VERSE

Night was born of great delight,
Night was rolled for the pleasure of gods,
Night gave birth to the split-back turtle.
Watch in the night for the land turtle.
Night gave birth to the brown lobster,
The night of commotion for the Alii (?) lobster,
The birth night of the lazy monster
Was a wet night for the rolling monster.
Night gave birth to clinging beings,
And Night loudly called for roughness.

Night gave birth to wailing
A night of drawback to oblivion,
Night gave birth to high noses,
Night dug deep for jelly fish,
Night gave birth to slush,
So the night must wait for motion.

Third Verse

Man by Waiololi, woman by Waiolola,
The earth was born and lived by the sea;
Guarded by the Kuhonua that grew in land (a shrub).
A night of flight by noises
Through a channel; the la-i is food, and creeps.

Fourth Verse

Man by Waiololi, woman by Waiolola,
The Wili was born and lived in the sea;
Guarded by the Wiliwili that grew on land (tiger's claws tree).
A night of flight by noises
Through a channel; la-i is food, and creeps;
So the gods may enter, but not man.

Fifth Verse

Man by Waiololi, woman by Waiolola,
The Aio was born and lived in the sea;
Guarded by the Naio that grew in the forest (mock sandalwood).
A night of flight by noises
Through a channel; la-i is food, and creeps;
So the gods may enter, but not man.

Sixth Verse

Man was created by Waiololi, woman by Waiolola,
The Okea was born and lived in the sea;
Guarded by the Ahakea that grew in the forest.

A night of flight by noises
Through a channel; the la-i is food, and creeps;
So the gods may enter, but not man.

SEVENTH VERSE

Man by Waiololi, woman by Waiolola,
The Wawa was born and lived in the sea;
Guarded by the Wanawana that lived in the forest.
A night of flight by noises
Through a channel, la-i is food, and creeps;
So the gods may enter, but not man.

EIGHTH VERSE

Man by Waiololi, woman by Waiolola,
The Nene was born and lived in the sea (geese);
Guarded by the Manene that lived in the forest (weed).
A night of flight by noises
Through a channel; la-i is food, and creeps;
So the gods may enter, but not man.

NINTH VERSE

Man by Waiololi, woman by Waiolola,
The Liko was born and lived in the sea;
Guarded by the Piko that grew in the forest.
A night of flight by noises
Through a channel; the la-i is food, and creeps;
So the gods may enter, but not man.

TENTH VERSE

Man by Waiololi, woman by Waiolola,
The Okeope was born and lived in the sea;
Guarded by the Oheohe that grew in the forest (bamboo).
A night of flight by noises
Through a channel; la-i is food and creeps;
So the gods may enter, but not man.

Eleventh Verse

Man by Waiololi, woman by Waiolola,
The Nananana was born and lived in the sea (spider);
Guarded by the Nonanona that lived in the forest (ants).
A night of flight by noises
Through a channel; la-i is food, and creeps;
So the gods may enter, but not man.

Twelfth Verse

The dancing motion till creeping crept
With long and waving lengthy tail,
And with humpy lumpy lashes sweeps
And trails along in filthy places.
These live on dirt and mire;
Eat and rest, eat and throw up;
They exist on filth, are low-born beings,
Till to earth they become a burden
Of mud that's made,
Made unsafe, until one reels
And is unsteady.,
Go thou to the land of creepers,
Where families of creepers were born in one night.
                    'Tis night.

The Fifth Era

First Verse

The advance of age when Kapokanokano (night of strength)
Established heaps in the Polalouli (depth of night),
And the dark fresh color of the earth thrown up
Was the darkness of the famous Polalouli (night in the deep),
Who married for wife Kapokanokano.
His snout was of great size and with it dug the earth;
He dug until he raised a great mound,
He raised a hill for his gods,
A hill, a precipice in front,
For the offspring of a pig which was born;
Built a house and paid the forest
And rested by the patches of Loiloa,
   For Umi who is to possess the land,
   For Umi who is to reign anon;
The land where Kapokanokano dwelt,
To which place laid a path of frailest trail,
A trail as fine as the choicest hair of this pig,
A being was born half pig, half god,
At the time of life of Kapokanokano,
Who became the wife of Polalouli.
   Night was born.

Second Verse

The Poowaawaa was born, his head was uneven.
The Poopahapaha was born, his head was flat and spread.
The Poohiwahiwa was born, he appeared noble.
The Poohaole was born, he became a haole (foreigner).
The Poomahakea was born, his skin was fair.
The Pooapahu was born, was a hairy man.
The Poomeumeu was born, is a short man.
The Poouli was born, is dark complexioned.
The Hewahewa was born, and he remained so (light-headed).
The Lawalawa was born, becomes a lawalawa.

The Hooipo was born, and became hooipoipo (loving).
The Hulu was born, and became a-aia (demented).
The Hulupii was born, and became piipii (curly-headed).
The Meleuli was born, and became melemele (yellow-haired).
The Haupo was born, and became hauponuinui (noble-chested).
The Hilahila was born, and became hilahila (very bashful).
The Kenakena was born, and became kenakena (bitter).
The Luheluhe was born, and became luheluhe (limber).
The Awaawa was born, and became awaawa (sour disposed).
The Aliilii was born, and became liilii (puny).
The Makuakua was born, and became kuakua (great).
The Halahala was born, decorated with lei Hala.
The Eweewe was born, who was proud of his pedigree.
The Huelo Maewa was born, with very long tail.
The Hulu liha was born, and became lihelihe (hairy eggs).
The Pukaua was born, and became a warrior.
The Meheula was born, and became red.
The Puuwelu was born, and became weluwelu (ragged).
That is his, this is in shreds.
Then came the children of Loiloa,
And the land grew and spread,
And the goblet of wish was lowered
Of affections for the tribe of relations,
Of songs that grasp of Oma's friends
Till relations are enrolled from Kapokanokano
                    At yester eve.
                        'Tis night.

The Sixth Era

A sacred emblem is the kahili of Kuakamano
That sends out its stiff branches as a sacred frill,
Which fills the faint-hearted with awe,
But brings such ones to claim friendship.
Those are beings who eat by gushing waters,
Who eat also by the dashing sea,
They live in nests inside ditches,
There in hollow places the parent rats dwell,
There huddle together the little mice.
It is they who keep the changes of the month.

The mites of the land,
The mites of the water,
'Tis Mehe the reddish seaweed
Whose lashes stand,
That hides and peeps.
There are rats inland, there are rats at sea.
There are also rabbits
That were born in the night of the crash—
They were born in the night that moved away.
The tiniest mice move by crawling;
The tiny mice spring as they move.
They run over the pebbles,
The propagating pebbles where no inland ohia bear.
A puny child born in the night of the crash.
They gave birth to beings that leaped in the night, that moved away
The child of Uli-a-kama last night.
                              'Tis night.

THE SEVENTH ERA

Over the mountains silence reigns—
The silence of night that has moved away,
And the silence of night that cometh,
The silence of night filled with people,
And the silence of night of dispersing.
'Tis fearful the steps and narrow trails—
'Tis fearful the amount eaten and left—
'Tis fearful the night past and gone,
The awful stillness of the night that came—
The night that went by and brought forth an offspring,
That offspring a dog,
A yellow dog, a tiny dog,
A dog without hair, sent by the gods,
A dog sent for sacrifice.
A speckled bird was first sacrificed,
Else he'd repent for having no hair,
Else he'd repent for having no covering,
And go naked on the road to Malama,
The easiest path for children,
From great to small,
From tall to short,
He is equal to the blowing breeze,
The younger brother of the god
From which sprang the gods of the bats—
The hairy bats. Sprang the bat with many claws—
Sprang the bat and moved away,
That the rising surf might give it birth.
                                    'Tis night.

The Eighth Era

The child of Uli, of Uli of Ke,
The child in the time of numerous night,
The child in the time of riding distant surf in the night.
Beings were born to increase.
Male was born of Waiololi,
Female was born of Waiolola,
Then was born the night of gods,
Men that stood,
Of men lying down,
They slept long sleep in the distant time,
And went staggering when they walked.
The forehead of the gods is red.
That of man is dark.
Their chins are light.
Then calmness spread in the time of Kapokinikini—
Calm in the time of Kapoheenalu mamao,
And it was called there Lailai.
Lailai was born a woman,
Kii was born a man.
Kane a god was born.
Kanaloa was born a god, the great Kaheehaunawela (Octopus).
                                        'Tis day.

The drums were born,
Called Moanaliha.
Kawaomaaukele came next.
The last was Kupololiilialiimuaoloipo,
A man of long life and very high rank.
O night! O God of Night!
O kupa, Kupakupa kupa, the settler!
Then Kupakupa the settler, the woman who sat sideway,
That woman was Lailai of the distant night,
Lailai, the woman. Kapokinikini
Dwelt with people of Kapokinikini.
Hahapoele was born a woman,
Hapopo was born a woman.

Maila was born and called Lopalapala (ingenious),
Her other name was void or nakedness,
And lived in the land of Lua (deep hole).
So the place was called Olohelohe lua.
Then Olohelohe was born in the day a man,
And Olohelohe was born at the time, a woman,
And lived with Kane.
Laiolo was born by Kane.
Kapopo was born a woman,
Poelei and Poelea were born twins.
After them was born Wehiloa.
From them these were born,
The little beings who were cross-eyed,
That stood in numbers and moved in myriads.
These men that flew naked were the men of the day.
                              'Tis day

THE NINTH ERA

Lailai, of the quaking earth,
Of great heat and noise, and opening heavens,
This woman ascending to heaven,
Climbed to heaven by the forest.
Onehenehe flew where the earth rose.
Children of Kii that were born from the brain,
Were born and flew, both flew to heaven.
Then the signs appeared and cast their shadow
On their forehead, a bread fruit was impressed,
On their chins shot roots of fire.
This woman was from a race of delusions (myth),
A woman with dark skin, from the land of Iipakalani,
Where numbers of men lived in the heat.
This woman lived in Nuumealani,
Land where the Aoa thrived,
Who stripped with great ease the leaves of the Koa;
A woman whose person was never seen,
From her to Kii, from him to Kane,
From her to Kane of Kapokinikini.
The times of those people came to naught.
A tribe, a generation of great strength,
She alone flew to her abode,
And on the boughs of the Aoa tree, in Nuumealani stayed,
Became pregnant, and the earth was born.
Haha Poele was born a woman,
Hapopo was born,
Lohelohe was born last of all.
These were the children of this woman.
                    'Tis day.

The Tenth Era

Maila, with Lailai for protection,
And Kane of Kapokinikini was support, Kii was helpless.
Laioloolo was born and lived at Kapapa.
Kamahaina was born a man,
Kamamale was born a man,
Kamakalua a woman,
Poeleieholo a child,
Poeleaaholo a child,
Then Wehiwelawehi loa.
Lailai went back to Kane,
Hai was born a woman,
Halia was born a woman,
Hakea was born a man,
The Muki, Muka, and Mukekeke were born (kisses, smacks,
    chirruping),
Smacks, boils, and other weaknesses,
Moku, Monu, mumuleana (strife, broils, and huffiness),
The men became speechless from sulkiness,
Became cross from envy of ours,
Of the woman who is brave and fearless,
Then hid and dared not claim kin,
To claim kin with her child.
The heavens deny the right of kin (being of younger branch),
Yield the sacred right to Kii;
For to be with Kii, 'tis his to claim.
Kane then taunts her eldest for this,
Kii retaliates through Lailai for his being the younger branch;
He flings a stone and hits Kane;
Then is heard the sound of the drum,
The sign of life for the younger.
Kane, furious with jealous anger, struck her for faithlessness
For the younger child of the younger branch.
That is why first-born are always hakus (superiors, lords),
First through Lailai, next by Kii,
Their first-born with sacred birthright
                                    Is born.

THE ELEVENTH ERA

She that lived in the heavens and Piolani (married her brother),
She that was full of enjoyments and lived in the heavens,
Lived up there with Kii and became his wife,
Brought increase to the world.
Kamahaina was born a man,
Kamamule his brother;
Kamainau was born next,
Kamakulua was born, the youngest a woman;
Kamahaina lived with Hali.
Loaa was born a man,
Loaa was the husband, Nakelea the wife;
Le was the husband, Kanu the wife;
Kalawe was the husband, Kamau the wife;
Kulou was the husband, Halau the wife.

The husband.—The meaning.	*Wife.—The meaning.*
Na'u (mine).	Kele (mire).
Aa (rocky).	Hehe (laughter).
Pulepule (insane).	Mai (sick).
Nahu (stomach ache, to bite).	Luke.
Pono (right).	Ponoi (one's own).
Kalau (the leaf).	Ma-ina (a groan).
Kulewa (stand in space).	Kune.
Po'u (wet night).	Kalai (clear sky).

These are myths of Gods.	
Poulua (Ulua night).	Kukululiulu (drops).
Pae (arrive).	Haaa (tube of roots).
Paeheunui (large hairy bank).	Kiekie (high).
Hewa (Sin).	Kulu (drop).

The husband.—The meaning.	*Wife.—The meaning.*
These are myths of Gods.	
Maku (thick paste).	Niau (glide away).

Wala (overturn).
Piha (full), pi-ha (dried branches).
Mu (moth or ogre).
Nawai (for whom).
Wawa (noised abroad).
Kuai (sell).
Luu (dive).
Mai (come hither).
Maia (banana).
Lana (float).
Lanalana (hopeful).
Pulu (wet).
Puluka (wet and dashed).
Pulukene.
Pulumakau (wet hook).
Pulukea (damp and light).
Nekue.
Nakai (the seas).
Kuleha (looked askance).

Kunewa (unsteady).
Pihapiha (frills or full to over-flowing).
Kuku (prickles, standing up).
Hele (walk).
Hanehane (spirit voices).
Aanai (grind).
Luulea (dove indeed).
Maia (by that).
Paua (rainy fence).
Kilo (foretell).
Paepae (steps of a house).
Lepea (turned over).
Lelepe (fringy).
Lelekau (leaped up).
Lelemau (leap often).
Umala.
Mahili.
Napoo (disappear'd).
Ma-ka (face).

Myths of Gods.

Ike (to see).
Mala (soreness).
Malama (careful).
Eho.
Ehoaka (cast shadow)
Ehoku.
Keoma.
Kinohi (beginning).
Ponia (crowned).
Meua (we).
Meualua.
Hoolana (float).
Hoomeha (loneliness).

Aoao (side).
Hui (together).
Puiki (embrace).
Pulama (make great deal of).
Pulanaia.
Malaia (stale).
Hahooili (landed tribe).
Muala (pebble insect).
Luka (drop and shake).
Mamau (held down).
Maukele (caught in mud).
Hoohuli (tip over).
Memeha (alone).

The husband.—The meaning.	Wife—The meaning.
Pula (mote).	Kua (back or to fall).
Kuamu (like a moth).	Kuawa (noisome).
Ko'u (damp).	Ko'uko'u (talkative).
Meia (thus).	Pekau.
Kawala (dash it away).	Mahuli (turn over and over).
Huli (turn over or to seek).	Imi (search).
Loaa (found).	Olioli (joy).
Huhu (anger).	Leawale (ecstasy).
Makuma (pimply face).	Manoa (thickness).
Manomano (persistence).	Lauahi (scoop together).
Kini (friends, many).	Mau (permanent).
Leha (glance).	Maua (two persons, we).
Pua (flower, glow).	Ena (shy, to keep away).
Puaena (bright glow).	Enaena (great heat).
Wela (warm, heat, burnt).	Ahi (fire).
Maiko (name of a fish).	Kulewa (beyond depth).
Maikokahi.	Kuakahi (single).
Maikolua.	Pahila.
Hilahila (shame, diffident).	Hoohila (act timid).
Kelau (tail end).	Lukau.
Paio (quarrel).	Haluku (dashing noise of water).
Paia (walls).	Kalaku (proclaim).
Keala (fragrance, pathway).	Kealaula (dawn).
Piao (fold up).	Naia (porpoise, fishes).
Niau (stalk in cocoanut leaf).	Kekumu (the foundation).
Launie (smooth).	Huluhe (dripping gum).
Mouo (buoy).	Paa (to hold, obstruction).
Hekau (pile on).	Kaili (snatch, skin).
Hoopaa (make fast).	Ha (to breathe through the mouth).
Kalama (Lama tree).	Kapala (smirch, leavings).
Helu (count).	Namu (bugbear).
Paila (boiling, a pile, heap).	Opuopu (filled to overflowing).

The husband.—The meaning.	Wife.—The meaning.
Halale (noise, swashing waves).	Malu (shade, protection).
Malie (calm).	Kalino (a rope for hanging).

Maoki (streak).
Kaiwi (the bone).
Kulea.
Makou (us, healthy complexion).
Ia'u (me).
Iaka (a shadow).
Makili (wrench from, parted).
Heamo (suck, bring on the shoulder).
Heamokau (stick for carrying bundles).
Puili (embrace, clasp).
Puiiliili (frequent embraces).
Puiliaku (hold on to it, catch it).
Mokukapewa (cut the tail of a fish).
Mokukaia (the fish is cut).
Piala (sprinkle water on the rocks).
Kiamo (any material used for filling cracks, napkin).
Koikua (falseness, to go back of).
Koiele (swing).
Paele (daubed with black).
Keomo (plug).
Hulimakani (change of wind).

Hulahe.
Iwia.
Kulia (stand firmly).
Koula (red sugar cane).
Mahea (where).
Meia (that's it, with that person).
Lulu (contribute, shake, calm).
Lou (hook, a wink of the eye).
Makea (barren country).
Apomai (embrace one).
Liilii (tiny bits).
Heleihea (go where).
Naalo (the two fronts).
Naele (two blacks, miry).
Heleua (walk in the rain).
Komo (enter).
Keaho (the breath).
Kauhi (the coverlet, a yam).
Peleiomo (Pele's sudden disappearance).
Omoomo (suck).
Nanailuna (look upwards).

The husband—The meaning.

Nanaikala (look at the sun).
Kalawela (the hot day).
Kealakau (a high path).
Kamau (luncheon, follow up).
Opala (rubbish).
Hali (carry).
Haliluna (take up).
Halimau (carry often).
Halipau (carry the last).
Nunua (pile upon pile).
Nananaka (cracks).
Oamio (hidden beneath).
Omiomio (things with small tips).

Wife.—The meaning.

Haipule (devout).
Kalahuiwale (forgiveness).
Hoku (star).
Meu (blunt).
Wene.
Halima.
Halilalo (take down).
Halelo (smutty).
Muakau (the first of the season).
Nenee (stunted, creep).
Leleio (fly and disappear suddenly).
Ololi (narrow).

Aila (eaten by the heat of the sun).
Ailamua (first eaten by the sun).
Ailakau (permanently burnt by the sun).
Ailapau (the last burning of the sun.)
Manu (bird)
Lilio (taut, drawn back or forward).
Leheluhe (hanging lip).
Kelemau (constant dampness).
Kaumau (always up, on an elevation).
Kaukahi (elevated alone).
Mauka (on land, toward the mountain).

Wiwini (pointed).
Kukala (proclaim).
Heia (entombed, caught, chased).
Hele (go or went).
Kaiwi (the bones).
Heleupa (walk and clash the knees or heels).
Makini.
Aina (land).
Hinapu (fall together).
Puoho (awakened).
Maele (cramped).
Kai (sea).

The husband—The meaning.

Ohi (gather).
Ikamu (little people, midgets).
Kalu (cleaning taro patch).
Kalukalu (name of a grass at Kauai).
Lipo (darkness).
Lipowao (dark forest).
Pili (be together, a grass, to bet).
Pilimau (constantly together).
Kahale (the house).
Kahaleai (eating-house).
Lawaia (to fish, or bird catcher).
Mauaka (two shadows).
Wana (sea egg).
Wanawana (ragged edge).
Wanakaulani (wana in the heavens).
Wanamelu (decomposed wana).
Kaulua (double canoe, two).
Walaau (noisy).
Hanehane (voices from spirit land).

Wife.—The meaning.

Laulau (gathered in a bundle).
Namu (little people, midgets).
Moena (mat).
Hilipo (thrash the night, wander in the night).
Na-o (mucus, phlegm).
Naele (swampy).
Aiku (toughened).
Maumaua (to retain).
Mua (first).
Nuu (eat with relish).
Kaio (a bird, flesh, disappearance).
Lehu (ashes).
Kala (a bird, the sun, a fish).
Wanakau (hanging wana).
Melu (soft, spongy).
Hulili (glisten in the sun).
Kaohi (hold back, gather).
Eiaau (here I am).
Hahane.
Kuamu (god fond of red color).

Hawane (Hawaiian palm).
Heleau (I go).
Hulimea (seek something).
Hulimua (seek first).
Ewa (uneven, district in Oahu).
Omali (sickly, feeble).

Maaku (to sling with a stone).
Aiko (eat sugar-cane).
Newa (stagger, a club).
Ewæwa (make faces).
Malimali (entice with flattery).

The husband.—The meaning.	*Wife.—The meaning.*
Huelo (tail).	Kakai (range).
Niolo (long and slight, wiry).	Eiaku (there it is).
Pilimai (cling to me).	Kona (his, its, south wind).
Keanu (the cold).	Peleau (name of a place).
Kaio (a piece of fish, a bird).	Pueo (owl).
Huluaka (old feather).	Kaolo (baggy).
Kapuhi (the eel, a favorite).	Mula (a bugbear).
Ehio (to lean).	Emio (taken secretly).
Kakai (range of mountain, straps).	Alakai (lead).
Amo (to shoulder anything, carry).	Koikoi (heavy).
Amoaku (carry it away).	Kuwala (somersault).
Helemai (come here).	Heleaku (go hence).
Onaho.	Keanalii (the chief's cave).
Pilikoa (mollusk).	Ukulii (a mite).
Mahinahina (name of a land).	Halepoi (house cover).
Poopoo (deep hole).	Nawai (by whom).
Omana.	Manamana (fingers).
Omanaio.	Huluheu (hairy down).
Manainai (flat).	Malanai (name of a wind).
Huluemau.	Kaalo (passed by).
Kaluli (rolling motion).	Pau (finished).
Nakino (those bodies).	Kinohi (beginning).
Nakinolua (two bodies).	Ewalu (eight).
Ukiki (small, stunted).	Eau (quickly, to swim).
Uli (bruised, dark, to steer).	Uliuli (darkness, black).
Mele (chant, song, to sing).	Melemele (yellow).
Lanai (veranda, an island).	Poi (praise, exalt, food).
Hao (iron, to grab).	Au (swim, tide, date or time).
Pakaikai (a weed).	Puehu (scatter, all gone).

The husband.—The meaning.	*Wife.—The meaning.*
Moana (ocean, on the deep).	Hilo (to entwine, land on
Hulu (feather).	Hawaii).
He (grave, it is).	Makalii (very fine, summer).
Makilo (beggar).	Hoeue (motion of paddling).
Naua (name of a society).	Moi (a high chief, a fish).
Ua (rain, shower, shout).	Upa (to slam, cut).
Peleu (broad).	Hama.
Mahina (moon).	Hamahuna.
Mahinale.	Hina (fall).
Mahinalea (moonlight enjoyment).	Ulukua (grew on the back).
Pipika (shrink from bashfulness).	Palemo (slip through, drown).
Mahele (to divide, share).	Kuhinu (besmear).
Kaohi (reserved, hold back).	Puunaue (divide).
Kona (his or hers, land on Hawaii).	Kaohiohi (hold back).
Iho (go down, downwards).	Konakona (disgusted).
Kulaa (his person is sacred during	Pelu (doubled, folded).
tabuday).	Mailu (not sufficient, little).
Kuamauu (grass on the back).	Holehole (stripped of bark).
Pahili (deceive, pretence).	Halulu (crash).
Keia (this).	Luluka (name of a chief).
Makioi.	Meihiolo (things that fell).
Helehele (cut up in strips).	Pineha.
Aukai (swim in the sea).	Milo (dragged downwards).
Moekau (sleep through seasons).	Helemau (go often).
Huluau (I take, name of a wind).	Pulama (brought up with care).
Melemele (yellow).	Milokua (returned secretly).
Kumuniu (cocoanut tree)	Pilia (joined together).

The husband.—The meaning.	*Wife.—The meaning.*
Amoi.	Akua (god, feared).
Kunewa (stagger).	Hulema.
Pahilo (delicate person, sickly).	Piliaiku (drenching wet).
Napoi (cover of calabash).	Kaale (ocean wave, swallow).
Kulana (unsteady).	Nawa (insignificant beings).
Kakau (an object before them).	Poipoi (smother fire or words).
Holeha (used for haole).	Hulupehu (swollen feather).

Paani (play, amusements).
Lewa (swing).
Pihaulu (full of balls or bread fruit).
Kelewaa (canoe steerer).
Kakio (boils).
Hulipena.
Mokiweo.
Kapalama (seclusion).
Kapalamalama (some ceremony of tabu).
Wikani (drawn too tight, too salt).
Kapehi (to strike, throw at).
Hiwa (anything precious is a hiwa).
Pano (deep darkness).
Opelau (many bundles).
Mahilu.
Hoolewa (swing, carry from place to place).
Kumau (firmness, large calabash, long-standing).
Papalele (flying board).

Malanaopi (fold loosely).
Kukelemio (hidden swamp).
Hoiha.
Kinohili (thrashed body).
Hiliha (to braid with four strands).
Miko (salted, preserved).
Pakala (small Kala, a fish).
Kepooha (the four heads).
Kepoolimaha (the four-headed hands).
Kamakolu (three-fingered mesh).
Kalukuu (the shaking down).
Kahiwahiwa (the precious sacred one).
Kekaliholiho (the choice sprig).
Maha (rested).
Kaena (boaster).
Waiau (swimming water).
Kahaka (ladder).
Mukala.

The husband.—The meaning.

Haole (foreign).
Makua (parents).
Leho (cowrie).
Opikana.
Helemaka (moving eye).
Kukuhale (beam of a house).
Pohakukau (piling stone).
Helua (counted).
Komokomo (ring within ring, entered).
Poeleele (dark night).
Nukueleele (dark lips).
Mama (swift, chew).
Hamama (open, to gap).

Wife.—The meaning.

Kuwahine (female Ku, sister).
Kaluakekane (the husband's second).
Holomau (constantly running).
Nahenahe (soft, flimsy, gentle).
Liko (young shoot of tree or shrub).
Hinaulu (growing Hina, growing gray).
Hinamai (fall towards you).
Kalani (the heavens).
Malie (calm, gently).
Hoolua (cook in Ti leaves, name of a wind).

Kuemi (draw backward).
Opiliwale (shiver from cold).
Ahulimai (turn to me).
Maikomo (nearly caught).
Hununu (humpy, lumpy).
Hoolohe (listen, obey, heard).
Kumaua (we stood).
Koikoi (begged, entreated, heavy).
Mauawa (looks after, frequent use of awa).

Papakele (wet board).
Pakapaka (coarse, rough).
Malele (not a pinch was given away).
Kulua (stood together, two).
Kapoulena (the yellow post).
Mahinuele (shiny black).
Pelemau (frequently, loose ground).
Kamanu (the bird).
Nawaikaua (whose are we? rain water).
Kulukaua (rain drops).
Hau (snow, dews, frost).
Kolokolo (to persist).

The husband.—The meaning.

Wife.—The meaning.

Kelelua (to dampen).
Makana (present).
Mahili (braid of strands).
Kukona (forbidding looks).
Kanawai (laws, to be warned).
Lohilohi (slowly).
Apikili.
Hoomaku (lowering clouds).
Olepe (oysters, thrown over).
Kala (forgiven, wrench open).
Hulipau (search thoroughly).
Makohi (dig, traces of footsteps).
Oopuola (live mudfish).
Niuhuli (upset cocoanut).
Ohao (fasten a dog, tumor in the stomach).
Nuu (to gauge, steps, upper grade).
Lena (stare, bilious).
Ahiahi (evening).
Ahiahihia (were belated last eve).

Aa (dwarf, fearless, root of a tree or shrub).
Mahiopu (motion of digging).
Wili (twirl, twist).
Naka (shake, tremble with fear).
Hapele (loose ground like slush.)
Hapeleau (swim in slush).
Nohilo.
Nahalau.
Makau (fear, fish hooks).
Heleaua (went with stinginess).
Hulimakeau (turn with the tide).
Hulimakele (turn to swampy place).
Nahalau (the sheds, large sheds).
Nakulii (grovellers, small stands).
Nakumau (the large calabashes).
Helemai (come here).

Ahiakane (fire or light of Kane).
Ahiakapoloa (fire of a long night).

Palemo (slip through, drowned).
Opihi (shell-fish).
Ounauna (hermit crab).
Wanaku (standing sea egg).
Kikala (the thighs).

The husband.—The meaning.

Wife.—The meaning.

Ahiakapokau (fire of night in the season).
Ahiakulumau (constantly dropping fire).
Ahiakamake (fire of death).
Ahiakaolu (fire of comfort).
Pohinakau (misty).
Moulikaina.
Hooku (to fit, to be made to stand).
Manaweulani (by the tasselly heaven).
Hoomailu (make small).
Mailu (small, insignificant).
Polehua (night of lehua).
Puulele (flying lump).
Hamohulu (brush with feather).
Iamama ('tis finished).
Kuinewa (blow from a club).
Holopulau (run altogether).
Makanewanewa (moving eyes).
Melia (with Lia).
Humuhumu (sew, to stitch together).
Ukianu (coarse grass growing in cold places).
Ukinala (coarse grass plaited).
Ukiakamau (coarse grass, often shaken).
Ukilelewa (coarse grass hanging).

Hapuu (fern-root, a mountain).
Makani (wind).
Kilou (hook on).
Honika (kiss with emphasis).
Hilahea.
Hoomaka (to begin).
Nanana (spider).
Laukunu (broiled leaf).
Puluea (dust of Pulu).
Lehuane (dust of ashes).
Keahu (the pile).
Noelo (insinuate, tease).
Noeula (red mist).
Noenoe (misty, foggy).
Pilimauu (flower grass).
Hinakona (he will slip up).
Helepuau (I went also).
Melemele (yellow).
Palamau (always ripe).
Nenue (a fish of the kind called perch).
Ilimaka (raw skin or hide).
Keohoko (leaves of sugarcane).
Laumeki (a kind of eel).

Ukinahina (coarse grass for Hina).
Hoopulu (dampen).
Nahiole (no fires).
Mukiki (kisses, smacking lips when hurt).
Kiola (throw away).
Mulemulea (bitter).
Kukawa (between times).
Kamio (to disappear).
Hoomu (left in a pile).
Hailau (to be sacrificed in numbers).
Hoomauke-a (continue to burn).
Kuaua (heavy shower).
Moeiho (lie down).
Manuala (that bird, sweet bird).
Kolealea (woman who leaves her child for pleasure).
Hilohilo (twine ropes).
Maluipo (shelter for lover).
Awaia (treachery on some one).
Hoohinu (polish up, smear with grease).
Eapu (to grasp or gulp it down).
Ialo (a front).
Heiau (temple).
Heiaumana (powerful temple).
Pulemo (slipped through).

Nilea.
Oloolohu (festered, bubbled).
Kealapii (the ladder).
Makino.
Ia-a (those rocks).
Helelu (walk and strew).
Maikaiwa (from the ninth).
Molemole (lag behind, roots).
Unauna (crab in a shell).
Pamakani (hibiscus).
Muli (younger).
Wailuhi (drink that inebriates).
Imihia (sought for).
Kawele (drag, wipe up, wave gracefully).
Kauwewe (rushes, put over heated stones).
Hokelona.
Hokii (sickly, consumptive).
Milo (twine, drag downwards).
Ohouma (narrow chested).
Uluoha (to grow finely).
Makalewa (hanging eyes).
Piioha (go up for kalo tops).
Hoohiwa (to make much of).
Maluolua (both in peace).

Kaukeoa (place the rafters).
Helemua (went first).
Kalele (lean on).
Paepae (pillow, door-sill).
Keoa (the rafters).
Kapouhina (the fallen post).

Hiileia (precious burden).
Puainea (something delicate and nice).
Wamakona (time of unfriendliness).
Limaauki (hand of ki stalks).

Kapouhinaha (four fallen posts).
Hoopiopio (sorcery).
Hoopioaka (make a curving shadow).
Hoolahalaha (make flat).
Hoomahilu (try to be distant).
Nanewa (the clubs).
Nanawaa (look for canoes).
Hookilo (pretend skill in sciences).
Kumeheu (stand on the trail).
Leleiluna (fly upwards).
Halekumu (house founded).
Halepaio (house of dispute).
Halemoeanu (cold sleeping house).
Haleluakini (house of worship).
Halekuamu (house of the goddess Kuamu).
Haiola (life offered for sacrifice).
Kalelemauliaka (last breath of vapor).

Puameli (honey flower).
Kuamaulu (tired back).
Hokuaala (fragrant shoulder).
Pionuu (curving ascent).
Pioanuenue (arching rainbow).
Pulau (applied to fishing).
Makua (parents, aunts, or uncles).
Peleuwao (Peles' protection).
Oma (oven).
Pilikamau (hanger on).
Leleawa (fly across an opening).
Mainahu (stomach ache).
Kimonaue (a game).
Holio (constantly before one's eyes or thoughts).
Keokeo (white).
Malii.
Noio (Mother Cary's chickens).
Laulaha (spread abroad).
Miloha (rope of four-strand twist).

The husband.—The meaning.

Wife.—The meaning.

Koiniho (axe of teeth).
Pooku (standing head).
Haleimiloea (house of science).
Panionio (many colored).
Kealakikee (the crooked path).
Oiaku (that's it).
Huini (name of a wind).
Pa (hit, barren woman, plate).
Pana (bow and arrow, snapped).
Panakahi (one snap).
Paikekalua (hit in the hole).
Puukolukolu (three heaps).
Napuueha (four heaps or hillocks).
Palimakahana (work by fives).

Naku (wallow, wade).
Paleamakau (ward off with fear).
Hilohilo (old skin).
Liho (something choice).
Maiau (natty, dainty, clever).
Kaniho (a tooth).
Naihu (the noses; the prows).
Aiano (it is there).
Koliau (I whittle).
Aliaoe (you go away, or stand aside).
Piliwale (to impose on your friends).

Waiakea (broad water).
Kaeamauli (Mauli's turtle).
Kokoiele (swing).
Kaholookaiwa (the flight of the Iwa).
Kalelenohinalea (the sacrifice of
Hinalea).
Panaakahiahinalea (first stroke by
Hinalea).
Panaikaluakahinlea (second stroke
by Hinalea).

Heleiamai (drawing down the
lower eyelid).
Hookonokono (to insist).
Helimaia (that is a hand).
Hepahuno (it has burst).
Eleiku (standing black).
Maumau (over and over again).
Heoioi ('tis pointed).
Aluaku (slack away).
Helule (limber).
Painaina (crackling noise).

The husband.—The meaning.

Wife.—The meaning.

Puukoluakukahinalea (third heap
by Hinalea).
Napuuikahakahinalea (fourth heap
by Hinalea).
Palimawaleahinalea (fifth heap by
Hinalea).
Akahiakaeaakilolo (first by the
turtle Akilolo).
Paluaakaeaakilolo (second by the
turtle Akilolo).
Puukoluakaeaakilolo (third heap
by the turtle Akilolo).
Puuhakahaaakilolo (fourth heap
by the turtle Akilolo).
Puulimakaeaakaakilolo (fifth heap
by the turtle Akilolo).
Akahi Keewe (first relation or
generation).
Palua Keewe (second relation or
generation).
Paukolu (third relation or
generation).
Puuha Keewe (fourth heap of
relation or generation).

Noakawalu (the eighth is free).
Piliamoa (leant like a chicken).
Manu (bird).
Lelekeamo (the shoulder-stick
flew).
Kelekeau (the fat gall).
Umikaua (tenth battle, let's
smother him).
Mailo (sickly, delicate).
Nihohoe (tooth like a paddle).
Paliiuka (precipice near the
mountain).
Paliikai (precipice near the sea).
Makaimoimo (winking eyes).
Lauohokena (that's a hair).
Pui (fat).
Nahinahi.
Kamehai (wonderful, strange).
Ulupo (dense forest, darkness).

Pulima Kaewe (five handfuls of relation or generation). Waiakaea Kaewe (oceans full of relation or generation):
Kamaulia Kaewe (hanging on relation or generation).
Koielea Kaewe (swung in relation or generation).

The husband.—The meaning.

Wife.—The meaning.

Kuaiwaa Kaewe (ground by canoes the numbers relation or generation).
Henahuno (it does bite, stomach ache).
Panakahikenahu (one stroke and then a bite).
Panaluakenahu (two strokes and then a bite).
Panakolukenahu (three strokes and then a bite).
Panahakenahu (four strokes and then a bite).
Lewelimakenahu (five swings and then a bite).
Paakaeakenahu (held the breath and then a bite).
Omaulikekenahu (all hold together and then a bite).
Koielehakenahu (four swings and then a bite).
Kuaiwakelekenahu (nine watery bites).
Hekaunano (only four).
Papio (to face downwards).
Manuakele.
Kaunuka (draw up the thighs).
Makii (flattened).

Newaiku (stagger'd from a stroke).
Puhemo (weakly, fainting).
Lahilahi (delicate, thin).
Kaukeahu (heap in a pile).
Ulalena (name of a wind on Maui).
Eiawale (there it is, they have arrived).
Konukonu (deep).
Uli (black, dark, bruise).
Nainai (shallow, prominent chest).
Pilomoku (bad odor from a ship).
Nahae (torn, slit).
Welawela (heat warm).
Loiloi (fastidious).
Kealo (the right side of anything, or front).
Kukamaka (pierced the eye or face).
Auhee (scatter, flee).

Kupololiili (dark night of changing pebbles).
Kupoka (so it is night).
Kupokanaha (forty standing nights).
Koponee (the night of your removal).

Haihae (traitor).
Milio.
Hamunu.
Naia (porpoise, the fishes).

The husband—The meaning.

Wife.—The meaning.

Kupohaha (dark night of feeling).
Kupoko (the night of success).
Kupo-e (suddenly dark).
Kupou (stoop down).
Kupolele (dark night of flight).
Kupololo (dark night of palsy or brain).
Kupolili (dark night of jealousy).
Kuponakanaka (dark night of trembling).
Kupohilili (dark night).
Kupohalalu (dark night of Halalu fishes).
Kupohelemai (dark night of coming).
Kupokalalau (dark night of wandering).
Kupolahauma (dark night of wrestling).
Kupoliilii (dark night of littleness).
Kupolonaanaa (dark night of cramps).
Kupolomaikau (dark night of chronic sickness).
Kupolohelele (dark night of flying Lo or being).
Kupolopaiuma (dark night of slapping chest).
Kupolohaihai (dark night of breaking).

Pakau (plate hung or put up).
Hemolua (loosed in pairs).
Naio (worms in food or water).
Kelekele (fat, muddy).
Hapulu (stem of a Pulu tree).
Napulu (that light substance found in a Pulu tree).
Kuamoo (path).
Muumuu (maimed, broken limbed).
Moonawe (slow, writhing snake).
Helua (hole, counted, worn out).
Poiwa (ninth night).
Nana (look, audacious, month).
Nakulu (drops, rumbling noise).
Eiamai (here it is).
Lelehewa (mistaken interference).
Kimopu (to fall together).
Holi (thin, slight).
Kupolupaiuma (dark night of scattering strokes of chest).
Luli (roll, turn one way or the other).

The husband.—The meaning.	Wife.—The meaning.
Kupokeleau (dark night of swamps.)	Makeamo (by the carrying).
Kupolonaunau (dark night of chewing).	Imo (wink, twinkle).
	Lua (hole, wrestle).
Kupoloahilo (dark night of Hilo, night of the moon).	Hulili (glare).
	Manu (bird).
Kupolomakanui (dark night of big eyes).	Hulu (feather).
	Namaka (the eyes).
Kupomaiana (very dark it became).	Pulupuli.
Kupolokahuli (dark night of overthrow).	Naku (wade).
	Ahi (fire).
Kupololili (dark night of Lo jealousy).	Hoaka (glitter, second night of the moon).
Kupololililili (dark night of extreme jealousy).	Lelea (to jump or leap, he leapt the fence).
Kupololalala (dark night of sun bath).	Hanau (give birth, was born).
	Ilimai (willed to me, a legacy).
Kupolohalala (dark night of reeling).	Hooilo (winter months).
	Makanalau (numbers of presents).
Kupololuana (dark night of a gathering).	Hulipumai (they all turned over).
	Leleiluna (flew upwards).
Kupololailai (dark night of a calm).	
Kupololaiolo.	
Kupoloololaimai (dark night of calmness coming).	
Kupololaiaku (dark night of calmness going).	
Kupolohilihili (dark night of strokes).	
Kupolomalimali (dark night of Lo seeking favor).	
Kupoloale (dark night of Lo swallowing).	

The husband.—The meaning.	*Wife.—The meaning.*
Kupoloimo (dark night of Lo winking).	Holookoa (whole, actually ran).
Kupolokalili (dark night of Lo with jealousy).	Uliuli (dark, blackness).
Kupolomene.	Hiwauli (precious one of darkness).
Kupolohulu (dark night of Lo's feathers).	Kinopu (prancing).
Kupolohulilau (dark night of search leaves).	Makaiao (watching of the dawn).
Kupolohulimai (dark night to turn backward).	Makiaoea (sickly fingernail).
Kupolokamanao (dark night of thoughts).	Ewa (uneven, make faces).
Kupolokeweka.	Lukona.
Kupolokulu (dark night of dropping).	Eapaipai (flapping tortoise).
Kupolonehea.	Hulihele (search around).
Kupolohaliu (dark night of facing you, or up or anywhere).	Maliu (listen to me, hearken to me).
Kupolonakunaku (dark night to wallow).	Uliau (I am bruised).
Kupoloololi (dark night of unevenness).	Holeaku (strip it).
O Polo (night of Lo).	Nolu (soft, spongy).
Polohili (Lo's night of striking).	Kau (put up, season).
Polokau (Lo's night of hanging or put up).	Uli (dark, bruise).
Polouli (Lo's night of darkness).	Polo (to pretend).
Polopolo.	Hamu (eating this, that, and everything, to search).
Polohamu (Lo's night of greed).	Nini (pour out, offended).

The husband.—The meaning.	*Wife—The meaning.*
Polonini (Lo's night of anger, pour).	Haihai (break into pieces).
Polohaihai (Lo's dark night of breaking).	Hei (caught).
	Hanuai (search for food).
	Ewa (uneven).

Poloheihei (pretending racing).
Kupolohanuai (stand and pretend to seek food).
Polomahimahi.
Poloaku.
Polomai.
Eliakapolo (the digging of the polo).
Ekukukapolo (the standing polo).
Halimaikapolo.
Hoopoloiho.
Poloku (night of danger).
Polokane.
Polohiwa (choice polo).
Polomua (the first polo).
Popolomea (something polo).
Popolohuamea (berries of mea).
Popolokaia.
Polonananana (spider god).
Polomakiawa.
Poloanewa.
Polohauhau (striking polo).
Polohehewa.
Polomehewa.
Poloulaa (overturning god).
Poloahiwa.

Kolo (creep).
Maluape (protecting ape).
Pelepele (swampy).
Puaa (pig).
Puaakame.
Uluea (growing turtles).
Hiamanu.
Paka (cut off in pieces, tobacco).
Leleamio (leap neatly).
Halu (yield when pressed).
Menea.
Miomio (slick, prim).
Omo (suck).
Lanaki (float ki).
Manahulu.
Laohe (day of bamboo).
Peleaku.
Nanale (void).
Huamua (first word).
Hewa (sin, wrong, mistake).
Makolu (deep cut, measure three fingers).
Hiwa (choice, precious).

The husband.—The meaning.

Poloula (redness of the god Polo).
Polowe-na.
Poloimu.
Polokakahia.
Poloi.
Poloii (yellow polo).
Polohipa (strange polo).
Polohipakeke.
Polohi-pakaka.
Polohi-hele-hele-lahiki.

Wife.—The meaning.

Ula (red, bright).
We-na (red glow).
Mohalu (anything that yields when pressed).
Kanakau.
Ii (mouldy).
Hipa (odd).
Pepa.
Meao (something to pierce).
Lahiki (sun is come).

Polohi-paukahiki.
Polohilele.
Poloahaumea (Haumea's polo night).
Poloahiluna (fire god above).
Polokaumai (Polo's night above).
Polokaulani (Polo's night in heaven).
Poloikamakani (Polo in the wind).
Poloikai (Polo towards the sea).
Poloikamehana (Polo in heat).
Poloimaumau (Polo of firmness).
Poloimauna (Polo of the mountain).
Poloilaau (Polo of the wood).
Poloikanahele (Polo of the forest).

Kahiki (foreign land).
Kaahiki (journey).
Haumea (a goddess).
Ahiluna (fire above).
Kaumai (laid on, lay it on).
Kaulani (on the heavens or sacred place).
Kamakani (the wind).
Ikai (at sea, bring some salt water).
Kamehani.
Maumau (over and over).
Mauna (mountain, hill).
Laau (wood, stick).
Kanahele (forest of trees).
Kukulu (build, implant).

The husband.—The meaning.

Wife.—The meaning.

Poloikukulu (Polo did build).
Poloihoomoe.
Poloihanahana.
O Polokahiau.
Poloikalua (Polo in the ditch).
Poloahiko.
Poloikaha.
Poloihilima.
Poloioaiku.
Polomauli.
Polokokoiele.
Polokuaiwa.
Polohemo.
Polokinau.
Polokii.
Pololii.
Polowaikaua.
Liili.
Liiliauau.
Liilikamau.

Hoomoe (laid down).
Hanahana (hot, excessive heat).
Kahaiau (temple).
Luahiko.
Hiko.
Kaha (large, fat).
Lima (hands).
Waiku (standing water).
Mauli (gasping).
Koiele (swing).
Iiwa.
Hemo (undone, wrenched, taken of, separated).
Nahunahu (in travail, bitten in bits).
Oliiloa.
Mano (shark).
Halula (sea eggs).
Pomea (night of things).
Auau (bathe, bathing).

Liililiili.	Kamau (to eat, to fasten firmly).
Liilihalula.	Holiholi (thin, slight).
Liilimama.	Nanaahu (inspect the tapas).
Liilimanua.	Hole (strip).
Liilihakahaka.	Holehole (as above).
Liiliha.	Pilimau (close companionship).
Liilihemoaku.	Hoohene (to make fun of).
Liilikaumai.	Iwiaku (bone of the bonito).
Liiliaolo.	Lahikama.
	Iliuli (dark skin).
	Oloolo (baggy, hang loosely).

The husband.—The meaning.	*Wife.—The meaning.*
Liilipihapiha.	Nuunuu (crimpy).
Liilinuunuu.	Helelinaa (walk on crags).
Liilihelelima.	Auli (whoredom, by Uli the god).
Liiliau.	Nolunolu (soft as down).
Liilimiha.	Haleakeaka (house of shadow).
Liilinanaia.	Puluka (stalk of the Pulu).
Liilipelu-a.	Maluli.
Liilimahimahi.	Makauma (eye for wrestling).
Liilikaliaka.	Nahili (put on a false trail).
Liilimelau.	Poloa (long night).
Liilileoleo.	Popoko (short night).
Liililimanu.	Poimoimo (blinking night).
Liilikapili.	Poiauwale (night gone without
Liiliholowaa.	incidents).
Liiliholomau.	Poilumai (night of strewing).
Liilikalele.	Poinanaia (forgot the fishes).
Liilikaili.	Onanana (pain of travail).
Liilipoipo.	Nanaue (looking askance).
Liiliwalewale.	Nahuila (the red fires).
Liilihanahana.	Meia (with him or her, so).
Liilihuliana.	Kulaimoku (overturn the ship).
Liiliwahipali.	Pihi (small).
Liilinohopali.	Pililau (enormous stakes on bet).
Liilinohoana.	Maeleele (numbness).
Liilikauhale.	Kauhale (houses).

Liilipulepule.   Palia (craggy precipice).
Liilila.   Pule (pray, prayer).
Liilihou.   Halawai (meeting, met).
Liilikakii.   Leleipaoa (flew at dead of night).
Liilikahuli.   Miliamau (fondle often).
                        Kulana (unsteady, position).

The husband.—The meaning.	*Wife.—The meaning.*
Liilihomole.	Iwaiwa (maiden-hair fern).
Liilipukaua.	Luna (upward, above, official).
Liilililulilo.	Kaua (we, us).
Liililanalana.	Lilo (gone, given away).
Liililanakila.	Kila (steel, seal).
Liililanaau.	Kilaua.
Liilimalana.	Maaa (name of Lahama wind).
Liiliahula.	Lana (float, launch).
Liilipukiu.	Piko (navel, centre).
Liilipaluku.	Hulikau (overturned on top).
Liilimaemae.	Pakapaka (blotches).
Liiokioki.	Liilii (small bits).
Liialiilii.	Lilioma.
Liiakauliilii.	Manukele (wet-bird).
Liiakamama.	Mama (swift, chew).
Liiamama.	Paepae (sill of a door).
Liipaepae.	Umu (native oven).
Liiumu.	Kii (image, went after something).
Liiluakii.	
Liiluakini.	Kini (1,000, forties, friends).
Liimolohi.	Lohi (late, slowly).
Liikauunahele.	Nahele (forest, woods weeds).
Liiaupa.	Upa (slammed, banged, slapped).
Liimuliawa.	Liawa.
Liinewaku.	Newaku (stood unsteady).
Liihomali.	Mali (fasten the bait with twine, deceive).
Liipulama.	
Liipalama.	Pulama (fondle, make great deal of).
Liiohinu.	Palama (seclusion).

Ohinu (to besmear, to roast).
Omaka (sprout, budding, sowing of).

The husband.—The meaning.

Liiomaka.
Liipau.
O A (light, on fire, some thing brilliant).
Alii (a chief, person of rank).
Aliilaa (chief dedicated).
Aliiaka (shadow of a chief).
Aliimau (always a chief).
Aliialii (chief of chiefs).
Aliipoi (chief made much of).
Aliikono (chief's invitation).
Aliipahu (stabbing chief).
Aliiume (chief that would drag you down).
Aliihala (chief full of crime).
Aliiponi (chief dedicated).
Aliilanahu (charcoal chief).
Aliikaea (tired chief).
Aliihonupuu (chief with throat like a turtle).
Opuupuu (full of lumps).
Aliilehelehe (chief with lips).
Aliimakolu (chief thrice the rank).
Aliinohouka (chief who lived in the mountains).
Aliihimuhani.
Aliileleiona (flyaway chief).

Wife.—The meaning.

Olua (you two).
Kaneiwa (nine husbands).
O Lii (finest, tiny).
Laa (dedicated to a deity or high chief).
Aka (shadow, laugh, but).
Mau (fastened, caught, things, more than one).
Alii (chief, person of rank).
Pohea (which or what, night or night of call).
Mii (clasp).
Pahu (punch, push, burst).
Ume (draw towards you).
Hala (missed, gone, pandanus).
Poniponi (very black).
Kelenanahu (besmeared with charcoal).
Kaekaea (palatable).
Hohonupuu (deep hill).
}Kaeahonu (life of the turtle).
Lehelehe (lips, talkative).
Hinakolu (thrice thrown).
Mauka (towards the mountain).
Haui (sideways).
Lopiana.

The husband.—The meaning.

Aliiwalaau (noisy chief).
Aliikuwala (acrobat chief).
Aliikomokomo (turning in chief).

Wife.—The meaning.

Kukeleau (I am drenched).
Manaaala.
Lupuhi (shaking eels).

Aliiaku (made chief of).
Aliinewa.
Aliikuhikuhi (pointing chief).
Aliikilo (chief of science).
Aliikiloloa (chief that saw in the future).
Aliikilopoko (chief that had no depth).
O Aliiemi (backward chief).
Aliikolo (creeping chief).
Aliihelu (chief who tells of his favors).
Aliiheluone (chief who dug sand).
Aliipuuone (chief who made sand-hill).
Aliikamanomano (chief fond of encroaching).
Aliihukeakea.
Aliipauku (half a chief).
Aliinana (staring chief, kind chief).
Aliikilokilo (chief of prophecy).
Aliikiloluna (chief astrologer).
Aliikilolono (chief skilled in sound).
Aliikiloau (chief skilled in swimming).

Ikuwa (swell of sound).
Mania (smooth, drowsy).
Lahulahu.
Loa (long, high).
Pokopoko (stubby, short, little bits).
Anana (measure, six feet).
Amiami (sway one's body backward and forth).
Lepau (point).
Lepeake.
Malamu (field of moths).
Mahakea (barren field).
Hoouli (to turn dark).
Pololani (night of Lo's in the heavens).
Kalakala (rough surface).
Huli (turn over).
Kelea (surface made smooth).
Halululu (rumbling sounds).
Kalahai (broken or interrupted day).
Kanamu (little gods).

The husband.—The meaning.

Wife.—The meaning.

Aliikilohonua (chief skilled in the earth).
Aliikilouli (chief skilled in prophesying).
Aliikilokai (chief skilled about the seas).
Aliikilonalu (chief skilled about surfs).
Aliikilohulu (chief skilled about feathers).

Heanaipu (cave of gourds).
Hoowili (repetition).
Ume (draw downwards).
Ohi (gather, collect).
Pelapela (filthy, smutty).
Oheohe (slight, slim).
Malumalu (shade, safety).
Lipoa (a seaweed).
Kanulau (plant sprouts).
Nahele (weeds or forest).

Aliikiloahu (chief skilled about mounds).

Aliikilomakani (chief skilled about the wind).

Aliikilola (chief skilled about observing the sun).

Aliikilohoku (chief skilled about observing the stars).

Aliikilomalama (chief skilled about observing the months).

Aliikilomakalii (chief skilled about observing the winter).

Alliikilokau (chief skilled about observing the seasons).

Aliikilohooilo (chief skilled about summer).

Aliikaanaau (chief skilled about hearts or thoughts).

Aliikaanamalama (chief skilled about dividing months).

Hoopulu (make damp).

Kakelii (belong to the chief).

Hulu (feather, down).

Lono (heard).

Kea (white, to be crossed).

The husband.—The meaning.

Wife—The meaning.

Aliikaanaua (chief who divides the rain).

Aliikilomoo (chief skilled about serpents).

Aliikilokua (chief skilled about one's back).

Aliikiloalo (chief skilled about one's front).

Aliikilohope (chief skilled about one's fate).

Aliikilomua (chief skilled about one's future).

Mua (first, future).

Muapo (future darkness).

Muahaka (future of war).

Mualele (future of escape).

Papahuli (overturned board).

Moolio (taut).

Kilohi (look backward with self-admiration).

Anapu (flash).

A-aa (veins).

Pehe.

Wanaku (pierced by wana).

Haina (betrayed).

Kulamau (forgiven repeatedly).

Hilipo (slash in the night).

Keanukapu.

Laapilo.

Hoohali (draw out to betray).

Nauia (that is yours; chew it).

Ipu (container, a vessel or dish).

Muakaukeha (future of pride).
Muahale (future of house).
Muahalekapu (future of sacred house).
Muaanoano (sacred future).
Muakekele.
Muahaipu (first to break).
Muawaa (prow of a canoe).
Muapoipoi (first to fondle).
Muakamalulu.
Muahelei (first to stretch).
Muakohukohu.
Muakahukahu.
Muaoma.
Muanalu.

Kahiko (old, stale).
Po-i (cover up the dish, cover of a dish).
Helenaku (walk shuffling).
Kaukahi (singly).
Lulu (shake, lull).
Moolelo (a tale, history).
Kapili (to join together).
Kahu (servant).
Anoano (holy).

The husband.—The meaning.	*Wife.—The meaning.*
Muanaluhaki.	Nalu (surf).
Muanalupopoi.	Pokii (younger in birth).
Muanalukalohe.	Nanaku.
Muanaluhaikakala.	Moku (island, cut, pulled apart).
Mualala.	Hoonahu (pretend to bite).
Muahaipu.	Apiapi (gills of a fish).
Muapule.	Mahoa.
Muahanuala.	Ahia (lighter color, how many).
Muaikekele.	Mulemule (easily offended).
Muaipoipo.	Akia (bit in two, a tree).
Muakalaikii.	Lena (yellowish).
Muaikawaa.	Auhuhu (poisonous shrub).
Muaiopele.	Laaumele (singing wood).
Muaiopola.	Laalaau (woody, branches).
Muapali.	Wahine (woman, female).
Muahoopo.	Kikana.
Muaunu.	Ui-a (beautiful or charming).
Muahai.	Kahuli (changeable, overturned).
Mualupe.	Elieli (dig, dug).
Muakala.	Moomoo (soaking and bundling of tapa before pounding).
Muawekea.	

Muahilo.	Kapu (sacred).
Muakahu.	Lau (leaf).
Muakahukahu.	Eiwa (nine).
Muaamama.	Hiliahu (weave the cloth).
Muaahilu.	Kaomi (press down).
Muaanoa.	Auwe (an exclamation, oh!).
Muaalealea.	Olopule.
Muainakalo.	Kaimai (led hither).
Muaohupu.	Kinika.
Muaikauka.	Niniha (cross, ill temper).
	Niniahu.

The husband.—The meaning.	*Wife.—The meaning.*
Muaikumuka.	Moemole.
Muaikaunukukanaka.	Mokukaha (wide cut).
Muaokalele.	Opilopilo (stench).
Muaokahaiku.	Meheia.
Muaokahanuu.	Kamanuhaahaa (humble-bird).
Muaokalani.	Leleamio (jump sprightly).
Muamamao.	Aumalani.
Muanuunuu.	Kahakaua (division of war).
Muaokamoi.	Holi (thin).
Muaokahai.	Haehae (to tear).
Muaokeoma.	Mano (four thousand).
Muaokepahai.	Opelele (flying bundle).
Muaokaoliko.	Ehu (yellow).
Muaokapahu.	Kapilipili (paste together).
Muaokahana.	Hapoe.
Muaokahanai.	Hunu.
Muaokaipu.	Ohekele (watery tube).
Muaumeumeke.	Pukapu (sacred couch).
Muaapoi.	Ponouli.
Muaahuliau.	Lehiwa (to admire).
Muaipapio.	Keleauma.
Muailoiloi.	Pohopoho (exposing the back).
Loimua.	Nanio.
Loikahi.	Pa-e (heard).
Loilua.	Pililauhea.

Loiloi.	Manukoha (chirping bird).
Loikalakala.	Kanaia (it is his).
Loiloloi.	Naio (worms).
Loilolohi.	Puhimaka (raw eels).
Loinuiloi.	Kalino (rope for throttling).
Loiloikaka.	Kalaniahu (robe of heaven).
Loiakama.	Poepoe (round).
Loiiiopoe.	Hiloauama.
Loiloinui.	Uhuau.

The husband.—The meaning.	*Wife.—The meaning.*
Loipouli.	Muku (short, stubby).
Loimia.	Leleiona (fly towards him).
Loiapele.	Haikala.
Loiahemahema.	Nakulu (the drops).
Loiakio.	Kukala (proclaim).
Loialuluka.	Hiipoi.
Loiahamahamau.	Olo (baggy, water jug).
Loioloolo.	Papaa (slab).
Loikolohonua.	Hano (asthma).
Loiipulau.	Mahoe (twins).
Loianomeha.	Kaloa (24th, 25th, 26th night of
Loikinikini.	the moon).
Loimanomano.	Pokipoki (a bug).
Loiloimai.	Kinikahi.
Loiloikapu.	Holiolio (passing objects).
Loiloikala.	Alohi (dazzling).
Loiloinahu.	Aheaka (it is a shadow).
Loiloipili.	Naio (sill, edge).
Loiahuahu.	Wali (ground).
Loikulukulu.	Walihooke.
Loipilipa.	Nohopali (sit on precipice).
Loipilipili.	Nohinohi (variegated).
Loihalalu.	Mahealani (16th night of the
Loihalululu.	moon).
Loiloilele.	Palimu (mount of midgets).
Loiloipa.	Kahiona (countenance).
Loipakeke.	Lukama.

Loiloipo.	Kahikahi (to rub, smooth).
Loiloipololo.	Waikeha.
Loiipololo.	Manini (a fish).
Loikamakele.	Hinalo (the flower of the
Loihialoa.	pandanus).
	Oamaamaku (schools of mullet).
	Lahi (a species of banana).
	Keleakaku.

The husband.—The meaning	*Wife.—The meaning.*
Loimanuwa.	Lahipoko (short banana).
Loikalokalo.	Pauha (disappoint).
Loiihiihi.	Kaheka (pits in the rocks on
Loihilimau.	seashores).
Loimoemoe.	Piopio (the cry of chicks).
Loipilopilo.	Hookaukau (about to sleep).
Loikoikoi.	Hooiloli (pregnancy).
Loikoiii.	Puapua (birds' tail feathers).
Loiloloilo.	Mahiapo (work till night).
Loiloloilo.	Kulukau (hanging drops).
Loiloloikapu.	Kupee (bracelets, anklets).
Loilalolo.	Kealanuu (terraced path).
Loiloinaka.	Kinana (brood of chickens).
Loiloila.	Pulelehu (like ashes).
Loiloikopea.	Milimili (handle, fondle).
Loiimaumaua.	Apoapoahi (catching fire).
Loiikukii.	Pola (centre platform of a double
Loiimanini.	canoe).
Loiipukapuka.	Houpo (breast, bosom).
Loiomilu.	Kakiwi (plant slips of branches).
Loiomiliapo.	Polinahe (small stomach).
Loiomakana.	Ipulau (bowl of leaves).
Loiokanaloa.	Nahawiliea.
Loiokiikii.	Hoolaumiki.
Loiihiikua.	Palahalaha (flat).
Loiihiialo.	Hulikahikeoma.
Loiokanaha.	Kahiliapoapo (brush and catch).
Loiikeluea.	Kaheihei (the race).

Loiopilihala.
Loiomalelewaa.
Loiieleele.
Loipo.

Hilipalahalaha (broad braid).
Apuwaiolika (draught of water).
Ohiohikahanu (quick breath).
Palakeaka (stained shadow).
Mimika.
Kilika (thrash around).

Polaa (sacred night) was born.
Then Storm was born, the Tide was born,
The Crash was born, and also bursts of bubbles.
Confusion was born, also rushing, rumbling, shaking earth.
The sea became calm and mountains rose;
Water became lakes and formed houses;
With great awe the posts rose,
And shouts ascended when the spear of Kauikaho was flung.
He wrestled with Kanaloa, Kanikahoe.
Second night was born in the presence of Wakea.
Stormy night was born.
Plenty was born.
A fowl was born on the back of Wakea.
Then Kupololiilialiimuaoloipo died;
The Aukaha Opikokahonua died; he was a warrior.
The leaves bore and disappeared,
Disappeared in the darkest night.

THE TWELFTH ERA

The husband.—The meaning.

Opuupuu (lumpy).
Opuupe (slimy bowels).
Opuumauna (hillocks).
Opuuhaha (budding of taro flower).
Opuukalaua.
Opuuhanahana (rising heat).
Opuuhamahamau (beginning to suppress).
Opuukalauli.
Opuukalakea.
Opuukalahiwa.
Opuukalalele.

Wife.—The meaning.

Laaniha.
Pepe (crushed, humble, flattened).
Kapuu (the mound or hill).
Leleiao (flown at dawn).
Mauka-o.
Kilokau (watch the season).
Halalai (calmly).
Makele (swampy).
Opuele (black stomach).
Opumakaua (timid).
Lelepau (full confidence).

The husband.—The meaning.

Maunanui (big mountain).
Maunanee (moving mountain).
Maunapapapa (low mountain).
Maunahaahaa (low mountain).
Maunahiolo (mountain slide).
Puukahonua (hill in the earth).
Haakukui (rumbling sound).
Haapipili.
Kanioi (name of a poisonous tree).
Puanue.
Kepoo (the head, at the top).
A-aa (full of roots or veins).
Piowai (curving waters).
Nauanuu (grade in Naua).
Haulanuiiakea (broad glow light).
Mahikoha (noise of the Mahi).
Oopukoha (noise of the Oopu).
Hawaii (name of largest island)

Wife.—The meaning.

Makelewaa.
Hulipu (turn over, upset).
Kanaua.
Haalepo (dirtyish).
Haneenee (creep along, grow low).
Lalohana (low work).
Waawaa (uneven, rough, fool).
Haamomoe (all lay low).
Haakauwila (low lightning).
Lalomai (beneath).
Kau-a-wana (season for Wana).
Hooanu (to make cold).
Aamoa (tendon of a chicken).
Makohilani (grip the heavens).
Huku (a lump).
Hinahookaea (despised Hina).
Kumananaiea.

Kekihe-i.
Makuaikawaokapu (parents of the sacred fields).
Makaukau (ready).
Kalolomauna (brain of the hills).

Ulunui (luxuriant growth).
Kekilaau.
Ikawaoelilo (abduct while in the woods).
Hahalua (full of holes, ruts).
Kaloloamoana (brain of the sea).

The husband.—The meaning.

Wife.—The meaning.

Kalolopiko (centre of the brain).
Aa (clinkers, bright fire).
Kauwila (the lightning).
Palipali (hilly).
Punalauka.
Piheeluna.
Malanaopiopi.
Malanaopiha-e.

Kaloloaa (brain full of veins).
Wakaau.
Uhuihi (screen, to hide, to cover).
Palimoe (leaning precipice).
Punalakai.
Piheelalo.
Hikaulunui.
Pihaehae.

Kihalaaupoe was born a Wauke (the tapa tree);
The Ulu was born an Ulu (bread fruit);
The younger branch was born called

Kepoo (the head).
Oliua.
Kikona.
Hoopulupulu (made into lint).
Hoolehu (to turn to ashes).
Kaulunokalani.
Hoouka (place on top).
Kanalu (the surf).
Poi (food made from the taro).
Paepaemalama.
Kaulana (famous).
Palaau (picket fence).
Nukuono (sweet lips).
Pouhana (foundation).
Kaiwiloko (inner bone).
Leua (yellowish).

Halulu (rumbling sound).
Kauikau.
Kaimai (lead this way).
Auna (flock).
Lapai.
Kahele (the walk).
Aluka (in a crowd).
Hakihua (breaking waves).
Lenawale (turn yellow easily).
Kaumai (come aboard).
Kaulalo.
Paweo (look askance).
Hopulani (catch the heavens).
Hanaku (do as you please).
Kamaka (the eyes).
Kaoiwi (the form).

Hookahua (establish foundation).
Kuiau (I strike).
Kapawaolani.

Hoomalae (pretend).
Kuiaeonaka (strike and tremble).
Kainio.

The husband.—The meaning.

Wife.—The meaning.

Manamanaokalea.
Aukuu (kingfisher).
Kakahiaka (morning).
Kapoli (the bosom).
Kimana.
Polohilani.
Kahilinaokalani (the thrashing of the heavens).
Kapaia (the walls).
Kakai (girdle).
Oili (appeared).
Kapaeniho (set of teeth).
Kaupeku.
Kaopeopo (the bundle).
Nakia.
Koele (a noise).
Huakalani (heaven bore fruit).
Nuukoiula.
Kaioia (was pierced).
Kalalomaiao.
Hakolaoa.
Kekoha (the loud report).
Pipili (to attach one's self).
Kaulamaokoke.
Kaulakelemoana.
Hiikalaulau.
Hainuawa.
Laukohakohai.
Opaiakalani.
Opaikumulani.
Liahu.
Kanikumuhele.

Kaukaha.
Koha (popping sound).
Kuua (lowered).
Hoopumehana (warmed).
Kalimalimalimalau (the fifteen leaves).
Kalanimakuakaapu.
Hemua (the sprout).
Hoolawakua.
Manawahua (dyspepsia).
Mohala (open, spread out).
Okea (whitish).
Kapua.
Kukaailani.
Hoomaua.
Lohelau.
Kaunuuula (the red furnace).
Meheaka.
Meheau.
Hooliu (to be salted).
Kulukau.
Mahikona.
Ulukauu.
Kapiko (the centre, the navel).
Hoomau.
Hamaku.
Ulahuanu.
Hoolilihia.
Kumukanikekaa.
Kauikaiakea.
Kopohelei.
Hoomauolani.

Hoopililani.
Ohemokukalani.

Nawihioililani.
Kauhoaka.

The husband.—The meaning

Wife.—The meaning.

Pilihonua.
Hoomahinukala.
Laiohopawa.
Kuliaimua.
Laaumenea.
Hoopilihai.
Kiamanu.
Hoopailimua.
Nakukalani.
Naholokauihiku.
Pepepekaua.
Hoomaopulani.
Kukulani.
Kukauhalelaa.
Kukaimukanaka.
Kukamokia.
Kukahauli.
Kuka Moi.
Kukaluakini.
Hoopilimoena.
Hoopailani.
Lohalohai.
Kelekauikaui.
Kanikaniaula.
Keleikanuulani.
Keleikanuupia.
Keleikapouli.
Kelemalamahiku.
Hoohiolokalani.
Hoopihapihia.
Hoopalipali.
Mihikulani.
Maunaku.
Hooholihae.

Mahinakea.
Palihoomoe.
Kuaiwalono.
Hoopialu.
Mahiliaka.
Holiliakea.
Puunaueakea.
Hoopiimoana.
Kaukealani.
Apoapoakea.
Puhiliakea.
Ahuahuakea.
Awekeau.
Wakaaumai.
Hiliapale.
Hauli.
Leleimoimo.
Hooahu.
Puepue.
Kahiolo.
Mahikona.
Lauhohola.
Mokumokalani.
Meimeikalani.
Palimaka.
Pihana.
Opiopuaka.
Kuukuu.
Hoopalaha.
Hoonuanua.
Kukaalani.
Poupehiwa.
Kalelewaa.
Hinapahilani.

Piipiiwaa.
Kakelekaipu.
Nakiauaawa.

Naukelemauna.
Laulaulani.
Poiao.

The husband—The meaning.

Wife.—The meaning.

Nanue.
Hoohewahewa (not recognized).
Milimilipo (fondle at night).
Kuemakaokalani (eyebrow of the heavens).
Poopoolani (depth of the heavens).
Kailiokalani (the skin of the heavens).
Hooipomalama (courting months).
Kunikunihia (singed, burnt).
Paniokaukea.
Polomailani.
Polohiua.
Kukukalani (thorny heavens).
Hoolepau (deny outright).
Nuualani (steps of heaven).
Lanipahiolo (sawing heavens).
Hookumulani (commencing the heavens).
Hoonewa (staggered).
Lanukuaaala.
Hoopilimeha-e (deep solitude).
Maninikalani (weeping heavens).
Hoonakuku (moving heavens).
Lanipuke (clashing heavens).

Kuhimakani.
Hoopalepale (to push away).
Milihoopo.
Ohuku (projection of land).
Heanalani (heavenly cave).
Kiloahipea.
Kaikainakea (white sister).
Maliiluna (attached above).
Pokaukahi (on the first night).
Nakao (the shooting stars).
Heiheiao (race in the day).
Panionio (variegated colors).
Holoalani (passing heavens).
Pahiolo (sawing implement).
Mukumulani.
Newaa (beg for a canoe).
Kuaaala (fragrant forest).
Pilimeha-e (lonely companion).
Niniaulani (offended heavens).
Kalaniku (standing heavens).
Nahunahupuakea.
Kalolo (the brain).

The husband.—The meaning.

Wife—The meaning.

Ahukele (swampy).
Pioalani (arching heavens).
Miahulu.
Minialani.
Kumakumalani.

Oilialolo (from the brain).
Pioalewa (arching bow).
Pahula (dancing yard).
Kiihalani.
Hoouna (to send).

Hoopilipilikane (betrothal).
Nuakeapaka.
Palelaa.
Palimoe (slanting precipice).
Palihoolapa (precipice of ravines).
Palipalihia (mountainous).
Paliku was born (as a precipice).
Ololo was born (uneven), he was the husband.
Kumuhonua (foundation of earth).
Kane (a god) (first two were born together).
Kanaloa (a god).
Ahukai (last in birth).
Kapili (bound together).
Kawakupua (age of myths).
Kawakahiko (the olden times).
Kahikolupa.
Kahikoleikau (hang decoration).
Kahikoleiulu (decorate with balls).
Kahikoleihonua (decorate the earth).

Pilikana (relationship).
Holiakea (thin and white).
Palikomokomo (precipice with entrances).
Palialiku.
Palimauua.
Paliomahilo.
(page 66, from whence another line of Paliku branched off).
Ololonuu the wife.
Haloiho (peer beneath).
Holehana.
Kealonainai (short breasted).
Heleaeiluna (walk upwards).
Kapaulaia (this is the end).
Lukaua (cease war).
Kupomakaikaeleue.
Kanemakaikaeleue.
Kaakoakoaikeaukahonua.

The husband—The meaning.

Haakoakoalauleia.
Kupo (stood at night).
Nahaeikekaua (torn by war).
Keakenui (great longing).
Kahianakiiakea (open space for gods).
Koluanahinakiiakea.
Limaanahinakiiakea.
Hikuanahinakiiakea.
Iwaanahinakiiakea.
Welaahilauinui (burning heat of her beauty).
Kahikoluamea (strewing of age of Mea).

Wife.—The meaning.

Kaneiakoakahonua.
Lanikupo (the night of standing heavens).
Haneeiluna (slide from above).
Laheamanu (stench of birds).
Luaanahinakiipapa.
Haanahinakiipapa.
Ouoanahinakiipapa.
Waluanahinakiipapa.
Lohanahanahinakiipapa.
Owe (grating sound).
Kupulanakehau.

Wakea who was husband of Haumea, Papa, and Hoohokukalani, and
    Haloa was born.
                    Yes, 'twas Haloa.
(Wakea was the first man and Papa the first woman.)

A BRANCH OF THE TWELFTH ERA

(Turn to the 65th page, from whence this genealogy of Paliku began.)

The husband.—The meaning.

Wife.—The meaning.

Paliku (standing precipice).
Palikaa (rolling precipice).
Lakaunihau.
Nalaunuu (eaten leaves).
Kapapanuinuiauakea.
Kapapaku (standing board).
Kapapaluna (board above).
Olekailuna (naught above).
Kapapanuiialeka.

Palihai (broken precipice).
Palihiolo (falling precipice).
Keaona (to be taught).
Puukahalelo (standing heap).
Kainainakea.
Kapapamoe (lying board).
Kapapailalo (board beneath).
Kapapapaa (firm board).
Kapapahanauua (board that
brought rain).

The husband.—The meaning.

Wife.—The meaning.

Kapapanuikahulipali.
Kapapanuiakalaula.
Kapapakiilaula (the broad board
of idols).
Kapapaiaoa (groaning board).
Kapapauli (dark board).
Kapapapahu (short board).
Kapoheenalu (the night of surf
riding).
Kahookokohipapa.
Papaiao (board of day).
Panaheenalu (surf board).

Kapapaianapa (board that
flashed).
Kapapaholahola (spread board).
Kapapaiakea (wide board).
Kapapapoukahi (single board
post).
Kapapapoha (board of loud
report).
Kamaulikainaina.
Mehakuakoko.
Mauluikonanui (tired of greatness).
Hanauua (birth of rain).

Oliaikuhonua was born in the night of Puukahonualani.
Then next in birth was

Ohomaili (beautiful hair).
Mohala (opening).
Kahakuiaweaukelekele.

Honuakau (earth hung).
Luukaualani (showers that
deluged heaven).

Kehaukea (white dews).
Kahokuhookelemoana.
Mulinaha (last of broken birth).

Hinawainonolo (Hina of the gurgling waters).
Kualeikahu (back that bore his follower).
Hinawaioki (Hina of the cutting waters).
Ipoi (held up).

Then was born

Laumiha, the woman that dwelt with Kekahakualani.
Kahaula, the woman that dwelt with Kuhulihonua.
Kahakauakoko, the woman that dwelt with Kulaniehu.
Haumea who dwelt with Kanaloaakua.
Kukauakahi, the man who dwelt with Kuaimehana.
Kauahulihonua.
Hinamanouluae.
Huhune.
Haunuu.
Haulani.

Hikapuanaiea.   Haumea was discovered.

Haumea of mythical form, Haumea with eight different forms,
Haumea of several forms, Haumea in form of a shark.
Whose many forms took different shapes,
And at the birth of Hikapuanaiea her breasts were caught by the
        heavens.
This woman of Nuumea was discovered by a dog.
Nuumea was the land, Nuupapakini the earth,
Where Haumea's grandchildren increased.
In Kio sickness ended, the brains began to roll.
This woman that gave birth from her head,
Children were born from her brains.
This woman of the darkest night, of Nuumea,
And lived at Mulinaha,
Gave birth to Laumiha through the brain;
Gave birth to Kahaula, a woman, through the brain;
Gave birth to Kahakauakoko through the brain.

Haumea was the same woman
Who lived with Kanaloaakua.
Kauakahiakua was born from the brains;
Her children were mostly born from the brains;
With great slime was the birth from the brain
By "Papa who sought the earth" (people),
By "Papa who sought the heavens" (chief),
By Papa the great producer of lands,
By Papa who lived with Wakea.
Haalolo was born a woman.
Accompanying its birth were anger and jealousy.
Wakea became false to Papa.
Changed the days and months,
Ordered the nights of Kane towards the last of the month
And the nights of Hilo to be first;
And established sacred tabus across his threshold.
Such was the house that Wakea lived in.
The food of the parent chief became sacred;
The Ape, so bitter, became sacred;
The Akia (sour) became sacred;
The Auhuhu (pungent and bitter) became sacred;
The Uhaloa for its life-giving properties became sacred;
The Laalo, so acid, became sacred;
The Haloa that grow by the edge of the patch became sacred.
Plant the Haloa, the leaves will grow tall;
So grew the sprout of Haloa in the day and
                              Thrived.

The Fourteenth Era

The husband.—The meaning.	*Wife—The meaning.*
Liaikuhonua (longing for earth).	Keakahulihonua (shadow that
Laka (subdued).	sought the earth).
Kamooalewa (serpent in space).	Kapapaialaka (board that's laka's).
Maluapo (shade of night).	Lapuukahonua (doubled up earth).
Kinilauemano.	Laweakeao (taken to the clouds).
Halo (peer around).	Upalu (tender, soft).
Kamanookalani (shark of	Kinilauewalu.
heavens).	Kalanianoho (sitting heavens).
Kamakaokalani (eyes of the	Kahuaokalani (fringe of the
heavens).	heavens).
Keohookalani (hair of the	Kamaookalani (quietness of the
heavens).	heavens).
Kaleiokalani (wreath of the	Kapuohiki (pile of ohikis).
heavens).	Keaomele (day of songs).
Kalalii (day of chiefs).	Keaoaoalani.
Malakupua.	

The husband.—The meaning.	*Wife—The meaning.*
Haule (fallen, lost).	Loaa (received, found).
Namea (those things).	Walea (comfort).
Nananuu (crimpy).	Lalohana (low work).
Lalokona.	Lalohooaniani (air, lower work).
Honuapoiluna (upper earth in	Honuailalo (earth beneath).
darkness).	Polelehu (dusky night).
Pokinikini (many nights).	Pohakoikoi (heavy report).
Pomanomano (many nights).	Kupukupualani (sprouting forth
Kupukupuanuu (sprout forth).	heavenly).
Kamoleokahonua (foundation of	Keaaokahonua (roots of the earth).
the earth).	Kanikekoa (report from the
Paiaalani (walls of heaven).	corals).
Kamoku (an island).	Panainai (flat bottom).
Mokulu.	Hiona (features).
Milipomea (fondle night objects).	Hanahanaiau (to make current).

Hookumukapo (beginning of night).

Lukahakona (shake of rottenness).

Hoao (betrothed).

Niaulani (heavenward).

Kupulanakehau was born a woman.
Kulaniehu was born a man.
Koiaakalani was born a woman.
Kupulauakehau the woman
Who lived with Kahiko, the Kahikoluamea,
To them was born Paupaniakea,
Who is no other than Wakea, or Lehuula, or Makulukulukaeeaulani.
After them came men with great bundles
Which were tied together and hung up in the night of Makalii.
The stars secured were hung in space.
Streaks of dawn were hung up with Kupoilaniva in space.
Rocking here and rocking there
Hung the bunches of swift offerings,
Hung the bunch of stars that rained in Wahilaninui,
Hung the flower of the heavens Kauluaihaimohai,
Hung the little stars of fighting omen,
Hung in tiers, hung Kahailono firmly,
Hung Wainaku, hung it firmly,
Hung Kikiula, hung Kehooea,
Hung Pouhanuu (the post of tiers), hung Kailiula (red skin),
Hung Kapakapa (edges), hung the Mananalo (insipid),
Hung Kona (south), hung the Waileia,
Hung Auhaku (composing period), hung Kamakaunulau,
Hung Hinalani (stumbled heavens), hung the Keoea (turtle clouds),
Hung Kaakaa (Open vision), hung the Poloula,
    Hung Kanikaniaula, hung Kauamea,
    Hung Kalalani (row of stars), hung the Kekepue,
    Hung Kaalolo (heap of brains), hung the Kaulanakala (resting
       place of the sun),
    Hung Hao (curious), hung the Aua (a fish),
Hung, twice hung, Lanikuhana,
Hung Hooleia (thrown away), hung Makeaupea,
Hung Kanihaalilo, hung the U-u (a fish),
Hung A-a (bird), hung the Ololu,
Hung Kamaio, hung the Kaululena (name of a wind),

Hung Ihuku (peaked nose), hung Ihumoa (chicken nose),
Hung Pipa (sneak), hung the Hoeu (stir up),
Hung Malana (unsteady), hung the Kakae (name of a place on Maui),
Hung Maliu (yield), hung the Kaulua (postpone), one of the months.
Hung Lanakamalama, hung the Nana (float), one of the months.
Hung Welo (trailing), hung Ikiiki (suffocating),
Hung Kaaona, hung Hinaieeleele (black Hina),
Hung Puanakau, hung up enjoyment,
Hung Hikikauelia, hung Kaelo,
Hung Kapawa (midnight), hung Hikkaulonomeha,
Hung Hokuula (red star), hung Poloahilani,
Hung Kaawela (red streak), hung Hanakalanai,

Names of the months.

Hung Uliuli (blackness), hung Melemele (yellow),
Hung Makalii (fineness), hung Nahuihui (the group of stars, Orion),
Hung Kokoiki (little blood), hung Humu (to sew),
Hung Moha'i, hung Kauluokaoka (accumulation of little things),
Hung Kukui (lamp), hung Konamaukuku (their spikes),
Hung Kamalie (calmness), hung Kamaliemua (the first calm),
Hung Kamaliehope (later calmness),
Hung Hinaonalailena (Hina of the glowing calm),

Names of stars.

Hung the Hiku (seven stars, Pleiades), hung Hiku kahi (first seven),
Hung Hiku alua (second seven), hung Hiku kolu (third
Hung Hiku hana (fourth seven), hung Hiku lima (fifth seven),
Hung Hiku oni (seventh moon), hung Hiku pau (final seven),
Hung Mahapili, hung huihui (cluster),
Hung na Kao (the goat, Capricorn).
Strewed the seeds, finest seeds of stars in the heavens;
Strewed fine seed of gods, the sun became a god,
Strewed the seeds from Hina; Lonomaku was formed like jelly,
The food on which subsisted Hinahanaikamalama or Waka,
Sought for by Wakea in the deep blue sea,
In the coral mound, 'mongst rough waves,
Causing Hinaiaa kamalama to float, a sprig,
'Twas flung into his canoe, she was thereby called Hina the sprig;
Taken ashore and warmed by the fire.

Corals were born and eels were born,
Sea-urchins were born, sea-eggs were born.
Blackstone was born, volcanic rocks were born,
Whereby she was named Hinahalakoa.
Hina wanted food and Wakea provided,
Set his gods up and well bolstered,
Set them nicely in a row;
Then went after Hinakaweoa to be his wife.
A fowl was born and clung to Wakea's back.
'Twas a stain, this fowl that grew on the back of Wakea;
Wakea grew angry and tried to brush it off;
Wakea, provoked and annoyed,
Shook it off, and it lit on the roof.
That fowl on the roof,
That fowl was a chief
That came from the seed of Kaeoeo
That climbs in space.
The heavens did swing,
The earth does swing
In the starry space.

The Fifteenth Era

Haumea, she of Nuumea that stood in loose ground
Of Mehani Nuu's thick sward at Kuaihealani at Paliuli,
As the deep darkness is the greatness of her rank,
The sacred lonely heavens from Kamahaikaua,
From Kamehaikaua, god of Kauakahi,
Who cut the sacred step, and cut the heavenly Haiuli,
Felt bitterness in his breast, anger and jealousy of his rival,
Landed on the island of Lua, of Ahu a Lua, and stayed at Wawau.
This female god, wife of Makea,
Was Haumea the great and fearless one.
A strange woman was Haumea in her life,
For she married her grandchildren,
And married her children;
Married her son Kaukahi, whose wife was Kuaimehani;
Married her grandson Kauahulihonua,
Whose wife was Hulihoma;
Married her grandson Haloa, whose wife was Hinamanoulu;
Yes, his wife.
Married her grandson Waia, whose wife was Huhune;
Married her grandson Hinanalo, whose wife was Haunuu;
Married her grandson Nauakahili, whose wife was Haulani;
Married her grandson Wailoa, whose wife was Hikopuanaiea.
Kio was born and Haumea was discovered,
Haumea was found to be wrinkled,
Very aged, with watery eyes;
Her form was irregular,
Was sour temper'd and crabbed.
'Twas Uaia who discovered that she was filthy.
Her back was wrinkled as well as front.
He stamped on her breast, which shook down the wall of Nuumea;
Shook the floor; her breast was like that of a dog;
Those breasts which raised high chiefs
Took deep root from this woman of the forest.
Ole was born the man and his wife.
Pupue was the man and Kamahele his wife.
Manaku was the man and Hikohoale his wife.

Kahiko was the man and Kaea his wife.
Luakahakona was the man and Koulamaikalani his wife.
Luanuu was the man and Kawaomaaukele his wife.
Kii was the man and Hinakoula his wife.
Ulu was born, Nanaulu was born.
Ulu was the man, Punuu his wife.
Nana was the man and Kapulani was his wife.
Nanaie was the man and Kahaumokuleia was his wife.
Nanaielani was the man and Hinakinau was his wife.
Waikalani was the man and Kekauilani was his wife.
Kuheleimoana was the man and Mapuuaiaaala was his wife.
Konohiki was the man and Hakaululena was his wife.
Waolena was the man and Mahuie was his wife.
Akalana was the man and Hinaakeahi was his wife.
First Maui was the man and Central Maui was born.
Crouching Maui was born, Maui with a malo was born.
The malo with which Akalana girded his loins
From which Hina became pregnant, and by fire brought to life a fowl.
An egg was that child, which Hina brought forth.
Her husband was not a fowl,
Yet a chicken was brought to life.
When the child cooed Hina asked,
I have no husband, yet a child is born.
A brave child is born to Hinaakeahi (Hina of the fire).
It roused the anger of Kialoa and Kiaakapoko (tall post and short post).
They are Hina's brothers,
The two posts that guarded the low cave;
They fought hard with Maui and were thrown,
And red water flowed freely from Maui's forehead.
This was the first shower by Maui.
They fetched from the sacred Awa bush of Kane and Kanaloa.
Then came the second shower by Maui.
The third shower was when the elbow of the Awa was broken.
The fourth shower was the sacred bamboo of Kane and Kanaloa.
The fifth shower was the edge of the umu (oven).
The sixth shower was the first rise.
Maui sobbed and inquired for his father.
Hina denied he had a father;
That the malo of Kalana was his father.

Then he longed for fish for Hinaakeahi,
Learnt the art of fishing, was sent by Hinaakeahi.
Go hence to your father;
'Tis there you will find line and hook;
That is the hook, 'tis called Manaiakalani.
When the hook catches land 'twill bring the old seas together.
Bring hither the large Alae of Hina,
The sister bird
Of the great fiery showers caused by Maui.
He is the great magician that caught
By the mouth and fins Pimoe,
The royal fish that raise commotion in the sea.
Pimoe was wooed and won by the Ina of Maui.
But pity sprang for Mahanauluehu,
The children of Pimoe.
They were taken ashore, eaten by Maui, all but the fins.
So Pimoe was saved by the fins.
Mahanauluehu was saved by the tail.
Hinakeka was abducted by Peapea (the bat),
The great god of the bats.
So showers in plenty were sent by Maui
Which scratched the eyes of Peapea with eight eyes.
They fought a battle with Moemoe.
Maui became reckless and fought the sun
For the noose that Maui laid.
And Winter (Makalii) won the sun,
So Summer was won by Maui.
They drank of the yellow waters to the dregs
Of Kane and Kanaloa.
By strategy the war
Embraced Hawaii, encompassed Maui,
Kauai, around Oahu.
At Kahaluu was the after birth, at Waikane the navel.
It dropped at Hakipuu, at Kualoa.
For this is Maui of the malo,
The wonder of the land,
               Yes! of the land.

Maui was the man and Hinakealohaila was the wife.
Nanamoa was the man and Hinakapaikua the wife.
Kulai was the man and Hinahoopaia the wife.
Nanakuae was the man, Keauhonua the wife.
Kapawa was the man, Kukuluhiokalani the wife.
Heleipawa was the man, Kookookumaikalani the wife.
Hulumalailena was the man, Hinamaikalani the wife.
Aikanaka was the man, Hinaaiakamalama the wife.
Pumainua was born, then Hema and Puna last of all.
Hema snatched the goblet in the scuffle with Luamahaheau.
Kahainui of Hema was born, Hinauluohia the wife.
Wahieloa the man, Hoolaukahili the wife.
Laka the man, Hikawaolena the wife.
Luanuu the man, Kapokuleiula the wife.
Kamea the man, Popomaile the wife.
Pohukaina the man, Huahuakapolei the wife.
Hua the man, Hikiiluna the wife.
Paunuikaikeanaina the man, Manokalililani the wife.
Huanuiekalalailaikai the man, Kapoea the wife.
Paunuikuakaolokea the man, Kapuhookia the wife.
Haho the man, Kauwilaianapu the wife.
Palena the man, Hikawainui the wife.
Hanalaanui was born, Hanalaaiki was born.
Hanalaaiki the man, Kapukapu was born.
Mauiloa the man, Kauhua was born.
Alau the man, Moeikeana was born.
Kanunokokuhelii the man, Keikauhale.

Lonomai (heard from) was the man.	Kolu (third) the wife.
Wakalana (time of straining) was the man.	Kawai (the water) the wife.
	Puia the wife.
Alo (dodge) was the man.	Mailou the wife.
Kaheka (ditches).	Kamaeokalani.
Mapuleo.	Painalea.
Paukei.	

Luakoa.

Kuhimau.

Kamaluohua.

Loe.

Kahokuohua.

Kakae.

Kaulahea.

Kahekili.

Hinaapoapo.

Kaumana.

Kapu.

Waohaakuna.

Hikakauwila.

Kapohanaupuni.

Kapohauola.

Hauanuihoniala.

Kawaukaohele was born, also Keleanuinohoanaapiapi,—

The woman that lived at Kalamakua,

From whence Laielohelohe was born and who married

Piilani. Piikea was born and married Umi; to

Kumalaenuia Umi, who owned those precipices from whence slaves
were held.

Kumalaenui of Umi was the husband of Kunuunuipuawalau.

Their son, Makua, was the only high chief (wohi kukahi) of the island.

Kapohelemai, his wife, whose rank as sacred wohi Alii and Honor.

So their heir I, the I of the Kingdom,

Whose power and right to execute,

And lord of the famed lands of Pakini,

Of the sliding Ohia and the weaving of the islands of Hawaii

To Ahu—to Ahu of I, of Lono,

Of Lonoikamakahiki.

A Note About the Author

Liliʻuokalani (1838–1917) was the last and only queen of the Hawaiian Kingdom. Born in Honolulu to a prominent chief and chiefess, Liliʻuokalani was adopted and raised by a chief advisor of King Kamehameha III. Liliʻuokalani was baptized as a Christian and educated at the Royal School. Declared eligible to succeed to the throne, Liliʻuokalani married John Owen Dominis, an American who was later appointed Governor of Oʻahu. After her brother's death in 1891, Liliʻuokalani ascended to the throne, marking the beginning of a brief reign with which she would attempt to create a new constitution restoring power to the monarchy and granting voter rights to the poor and disenfranchised. In retaliation, and with the help of Hawaiian oligarchs, American led forces overthrew the Hawaiian Kingdom in 1893, bringing an abrupt end to Liliʻuokalani's rule. In 1895, following the failed Wilcox rebellion, Liliʻuokalani was placed under house arrest and forced to abdicate, leading to the annexation of Hawaii by the United States in 1898. During her imprisonment, Liliʻuokalani wrote *Hawaii's Story by Hawaii's Queen* (1898), an autobiography detailing her life and appealing for her reinstatement as queen. In addition, while she was Princess of the Hawaiian Kingdom, Liliʻuokalani wrote the popular song "Aloha ʻOe," (1878) now a symbol of Hawaiian sovereignty and identity.

A Note from the Publisher

bookfinity™

Discover more of your favorite classics with Bookfinity™.

- Track your reading with custom book lists.
- Get great book recommendations for your personalized Reader Type.
- Add reviews for your favorite books.
- AND MUCH MORE!

Visit **bookfinity.com** and take the fun Reader Type quiz to get started.

Enjoy our classic and modern companion pairings!

Classic & Modern